THE
DIVORCED
WOMAN'S
HANDBOOK

ALSO BY JANE WILKIE:

The Sally Struthers Natural Beauty Book
(with Sally Struthers and Joyce Virtue)

THE DIVORCED WOMAN'S HANDBOOK

An Outline for Starting the First Year Alone

by Jane Wilkie

Illustrations by Jan Logan

WILLIAM MORROW AND COMPANY, INC.
New York   1980

Library of Congress Cataloging in Publication Data

Wilkie, Jane.
    The divorced woman's handbook.

    Includes bibliographical references and index.
    1. Divorcees—United States.   2. Single women—
United States.   3. Conduct of life.   I. Title.
HQ834.W58   301.42'84   79-24662
ISBN 0-688-03607-4
ISBN 0-688-08607-1 pbk.

Printed in the United States of America

First Edition

1 2 3 4 5 6 7 8 9 10

Book Design by Michael Mauceri

FOREWORD

Although this book has been written by one woman (a divorcee), it has been compiled with the help of many other women, all of whom have survived the trauma of divorce.

Their contributions amount to an encyclopedia of emotional traps, financial pitfalls, health problems, social mistakes, and job concerns. In short, the interviews with each woman have indicated her regret that, in the first year by herself, she "didn't know what to do."

It was difficult enough to handle her emotions. But there was enigma, too, in the problems of everyday life. Suddenly, there was no man at her side to share holidays, open jars, handle finances, have the car lubed. Answers to these practical aspects of life were not provided in books written for the divorcee, all of which centered on her psychological slump.

This book zeros in on the practical, giving step-by-step answers to problems, plus detailed charts to help you create order out of chaos. In essence, this is a workbook to straighten out your life, and if you will use it according to your personal needs, you will have cleared the decks of your cluttered mind, enabling you to begin building a new life for yourself.

I thank all my contributors for their concern about this book. They *are* concerned—they feel the project is a much needed support for the newly divorced woman—and because of their immense help, the author feels the book has, in a sense, been written by all of them.

We hope you will find it helpful.

—JANE WILKIE

CONTENTS

||||C3||||||||||||C3||||||||||||C3||||||||||||C3||||||||||||C3||||||||||||C3||||||||||||C3||||||||||||C3||||||||||||C3||||||||||||C3|||

Chapter One
SO YOU'RE DIVORCED. . . .

For most of you, it's been a rotten experience, and still is.

For a few lucky ones, you're bloody well happy to be rid of him. But the fact remains, you are alone.

For some—you self-sufficient women who not only have a thriving career to put your head into, but know all about plumbing, insurance, and Phillips screwdrivers (for those who don't know about the last, see Chapter Five, *Your Home*, under "Repairs")—many points in this book may seem obvious. But unless you have your eye on, and your tentacles closing around, the president of your firm, you too are alone.

The differences are many, depending on how long you were married, why you married him in the first place, your age, who initiated the rift, whether you have children. But there is a sameness for all of you. We assume you have received your divorce decree (we'll tell you later where to put that paper, and no laughter, please) . . . the legal procedures are over with . . . he's gone . . . and you are alone.

It's for the woman newly alone that this book is written. It is comparatively easy when a woman marries to change "I" to "we." When you must return to "I" it can be hell, and you will probably go through a year of ordeal.

We've promised to help you in the practical matters of life and will give it to you, chapter and verse.

But first, we recognize that you're in pain and not quite

ready to be told how to straighten out your life. You're hurting too much to think about credit, blown fuses, a new job.

So we want to assure you that we understand. You bet we understand! On a scientific scale of readjustment, the disaster of a husband's death leads the list, and divorce comes second. This compares with the trauma of a term in jail, which rates fourth in the poll of emotional crises. So if you're taking it hard, you're normal. Divorce is surgery of the mind and spirit and, consequently, the body.

In this first chapter we will bombard you with psychological advice that is brief and to the point. No lengthy harangues, no case histories ("Sue had been married thirteen years when she found her husband in bed with the baby-sitter . . ."). We will give you only the sum and substance of the knowledge we've gleaned from those who have been in your boat.

You should know that healing will take at least a full year. Some women begin emerging from the cocoon in as short a time as three months. But that's only the *beginning*. There are ups and downs, some good days and lots of bad days before you soar on new wings. If you are average, you won't feel reborn until the first year has gone by.

We'll start with moods you can expect during this first year. If you know what to expect you'll be less likely to go off the deep end.

You should anticipate some or all of the following reactions:

- You can't concentrate—on anything.
- You feel terribly sorry for yourself (all those years wasted).
- You cry a lot.
- You wander through your days in a vacuum.
- You can't sleep. Or you sleep too much—known as "blockout."

- You feel abandoned.
- Your appetite is shot. You may even have nausea.
- You feel guilty. Because (1) you think you made a stupid mistake to have picked *him*, or (2) regardless of whose fault it was, your marriage failed. (It's the *failure* that gets to you.)
- You talk to friends, endlessly, about your divorce.
- You're having an occasional drink alone. Maybe you've gone back to smoking.
- You are bitter about him, particularly if he's already running around with another woman.
- You've thought about taking a trip, but who wants to travel alone?
- The time of day he used to come home is excruciating. That's when the loneliness really hits you.
- Your home means little to you. You've begun leaving the bed unmade.
- The children get on your nerves much more, and faster, than they used to.
- At the market check-out counter, you are acutely conscious of how few items are in your shopping cart. You feel branded as a woman who lives alone.
- Sleeping alone is unbearable. Not only the absence of sex, but there's no one next to you. It's like being somewhere out in space.

So, you ask yourself questions. . . .

- How in hell are you going to manage with no husband, no job, and children to rear?
- How are you going to make decisions by yourself?
- What will happen if you get sick?
- Is all the rest of the world a Noah's ark, living two by two?
- Your daughter writes, your son phones. . . . Why don't they come to *see* you?
- Where do you go from here?

11

- Will you ever find another man?
- Why don't your friends call more often?
- What do you say to people who phone *him*?

If you feel these things, if you ask yourself these questions, you are reacting normally. Lady, you are *depressed*.

How Do You Cope?

At the very beginning, let it go. Feel sorry for yourself. Cry, if it makes you feel better. You're going through a rough time and deserve a lot of self-pampering. BUT. There will come a time when you no longer feel sorry for yourself, when you no longer need to cry. That's the time to *stop* pampering yourself and get cracking with the life ahead of you.

Know—concentrate on—the certainty that you are going to rise above all this, that in effect, divorce can be a beginning, not an end. Marriage made you immobile. Divorce is your opportunity to gather yourself to yourself . . . and from this comes self-esteem.

When you hurt the most, at the hour he's due home from work and it's time to talk over his day and yours, to have a drink or two before dinner (the "happy hour" is termed that for reasons other than reaction to alcohol), don't brood. Have friends over for cocktails, or go out. Go to an early movie, preferably a comedy, and have dinner later. Go to a gym class. Take a bike ride. Walk with the dog. Don't just sit there.

Please yourself. Heaven knows you've put in enough time pleasing him—or trying to. Now you are number one, so treat yourself that way. It isn't selfish, it's sensible. You know by now you can't please all the people all the time. You can finally ask yourself, "What about *me*?" If you do things to make yourself happy, you'll gain self-respect and look at yourself with new values.

You need friends, now more than ever. Treasure them; nurture your friendships.

Begin entertaining in your home. Who's going to miss the host? Ask a friend to tend bar while you take command of the kitchen. Invite not only friends—include neighbors you never had time to talk to, and maybe the market clerk or the salesgirl who's always been so nice to you.

It's important to open new vistas, and for this you need an open mind. Be willing to accept new people, new experiences and ideas. When you talk with new people, use the trick of journalists who interview others. Don't stop at "What do you do?" Ask people "Why?" Ask them "How?" You'll be surprised at the communication this technique inspires.

Go out. Go to lectures, civic meetings, concerts, museums, the park. Don't be nervous about being alone. You think you stand out like a sore thumb but in actuality, few people notice you are alone. (It's the same as when you have a head cold and think you look a mess and are offensive; the truth is that most people don't even notice.)

The first time you go anywhere alone, you have made the first step. And it's a giant step.

Try to find time to do things for others. The world is full of loneliness, and you take the edge off your own when you relieve someone else's. More than that, if you've made others happy, *you* are happy. Visit children in a hospital; read to them. Take flowers to a nursing home; ask the person in charge which of the patients has the least visitors. Write their letters for them. Are you really too busy to take elderly people for a drive in the country? Or to do the marketing for a neighbor who is ill?

Release your anger. Slam a door (one without glass panes, please), throw pillows. Even better, play golf, racquet ball or tennis and enjoy yourself as you destroy frustration by whacking at the ball. We think you can even show anger in social situations; you've compromised with him so long it's time you released honest feelings. Giving vent to deep anger clears the air.

In the event your depression gets to the point that the thought of suicide flits through your mind, learn how to shake off these dangerous doldrums. There are lots of ways to do it, and walking is the simplest. A brisk walk clears the mind of cobwebs, stimulates circulation, makes life seem a lot brighter. And it gives you time to adjust. Read. Not *War and Peace*, for heaven's sake, but light stuff—novels, mysteries. Listen to music, something rhythmic, cheerful: maybe disco, ragtime, or Dixieland. Music that sets your feet to tapping can't make you feel any way but good. Avoid romantic ballads and heavy symphonic music unless you're one of the rare ones who are uplifted by this type of music. Go back to playing the piano. You haven't forgotten so much that you can't reap enjoyment from this, and furthermore, it's a hobby you can pursue. Go to an art museum, an ideal place to be alone. Take a cold shower to snap you back to normalcy—or a leisurely hot bath to precede a refreshing nap.

If you haven't one already, get a job. Even in the unlikely case that he is paying you a fortune in alimony and you don't need to earn money, you need a job. Staying at home with your hair in curlers isn't going to provide you with new friends or, more important, give you a new sense of worth. That old quotable La Rochefoucauld wrote, "Labor of the body frees us from pains of the mind." Work will make you forget your troubles, for at least forty hours a week. For advice regarding how to get a job, and eventually a better job, see Chapter Nine, *Your Work*.

Resume your old hobbies, and find new ones. Don't forget that Grandma Moses first picked up a paintbrush when she was seventy-eight years old. If you've thought about painting or drawing, get started, perhaps just sketching in pencil in the beginning. Have you ever wondered if you can sculpt? Find out. For under three dollars you can buy five pounds of nonhardening clay. Start collecting—first editions, stamps (a

14

good hedge against inflation), candlesticks, shells, butterflies, *egg timers* if you like. And, as we suggested before, get back to the piano, or start with your first lesson. It's never too late.

Recognize that change is the order of life. Psychologists say that every life has cycles of change, that no one ever gets through it without at least one great emotional upheaval. *No* one's life is safe, secure.

Know that you will go through three stages in the healing process of this first year. The first is shock, and takes a while to shed. This evolves into anger—and once you've given vent to this, you will find a sense of acceptance. When acceptance is achieved, serenity will begin.

Develop your sense of humor, the very best support given us to get through life. If you can see the funy side of any situation, you'll take yourself less seriously. And taking oneself too seriously is a trap for all divorcees.

Know that women take divorce harder than men, yet manage ultimately to become better people because of it. As for men, *they* go off and get married again, because they can't stand life without a housekeeper.

If you have a faith, lean on it. That's what religion is all about; it's there to help.

Like yourself. After all, you've put in years of giving to someone else, you have loved, we assume you've been loved —and God knows you tried to make a good marriage. Once you can tell yourself you are a decent and likable human being, you will find it easier to like other people. And be able, once again, to trust others.

Make up your mind that in time you will forgive him. Until you do, the green worm of gall will be buried deep inside you. Forgiving is the first step to forgetting.

The foregoing are things you should do. Now we'll give you some don'ts which are every bit as important.

Don't brood. The past is over.

Don't make any major decisions for a while—such as selling

the house or going into debt for something you don't really need.

Don't acquire any bad habits. Don't let the house go to pot, don't let yourself go to pot. If you'll forgive the pun, that includes drugs—and alcohol. You've hit bottom, particularly if he chose divorce, and right now are a prime pigeon for self-destruction.

Don't entertain negative thoughts about yourself.

Don't be inert. Never again will you have such freedom to choose for yourself, to forge ahead with your life.

Don't let him come back. In this way lies more madness. In one hour you'll be rehashing the same old arguments. If he makes a pest of himself, call your lawyer.

Don't go on a diet. Not yet. You're in no shape to deprive yourself of anything right now.

Don't dwell on "if." "If I had . . ." "If he had . . ." As we said, the past is over.

Don't bore your friends with your woes. Too much of this can alienate all but the best of friends; everyone has her own troubles. If you have one good, close friend, you will of course spill it all out to her. But watch her eyes. When they begin to glaze over, she has had enough.

Don't take on new responsibilities that are either stressful or pressuring. Learn how to say no.

After a few months, stop feeling sorry for yourself. You may not know it yet, but the truth is that because you are divorced, you're free to be your own person.

Count Your Blessings

An old saw, but oh so handy when you're down in the dumps. We'll count some for you:

- Nobody's there to criticize you. Remember all that carping? It was destructive.
- If you hanker for an onion sandwich at 3:00 A.M., you can have an onion sandwich.

16

- You can choose your own TV shows and movies, plus your own *quiet*.
- If you're not hungry and the kids aren't around, you don't have to cook.
- You don't have to clean house, unless you want to.
- You can spend money in the way you wish.
- No more entertaining his business friends, no more addressing his business Christmas cards.
- When you're tired you can take a nap. And you can go to bed at night when you please.
- You can regenerate friendships with the women he didn't like.
- You can eat as you wish. No more turnips in the stew for him.
- You can wear what you like.
- You can make your own decisions. Perhaps tough at first, but afterward—beautiful.
- You can travel where you want to travel.
- You have privacy—lovely, peaceful privacy.
- A small item but cheering—you no longer have to iron his handkerchiefs.
- You don't have to explain your thoughts, your deeds, your motives.
- You can love and discipline the kids when you think it's time for love or discipline.
- You finally have yourself to yourself. Married, you were half of him. Now you're you, and can decide what you want to do with *your* life. Believe us, you will find a way.

This chapter has given you all you need of psychological advice in one lump. It's one helluva lump, but it's all there, without frills. Just the nitty-gritty of what you need to know in order to deal with your emotions.

From now on, we'll help you get you life organized in practical matters. After you've attended to all necessary details, your mind will be free to think about the future.

Recommended Reading

After You've Said Goodbye: How to Recover After Ending a Relationship by Trudy Helmlinger. (Two Continents/ Schenkman, hardbound, $8.95).

A counselor on family and marriage gives guidance with both common sense and a sense of humor.

How to Use the Charts

Beginning on the next pages, charts will follow each chapter in this book.

There will be two kinds:

(1) DO. A chart directly related to the preceding chapter. It will list the actions you need to take, followed by a priority column. Those actions we *know* must be attended to as soon as possible are marked here with the number 1. Priority of the remainder is up to you. For some you might wait weeks or months; others won't apply to you at all. You may want to gauge them yourself in the priority column with a 2, 3, etc. The next column, marked "Done," is where you may check each item as it's taken care of. The following pages will tell you how to accomplish each thing, unless the method is obvious. A final column is supplied for your notes.

(2) THINK. These are furnished because much of your organization will be thought process rather than action. The THINK charts give you plenty of extra space for notes. (On these, we may butt in with suggestions for your thoughts.) *Only* THINK charts are supplied for this first chapter, and for the chapters regarding your work and social life, both of which need to be thought about rather than acted on.

Full use of the charts in this workbook will leave your mind infinitely less littered with unsolved detail, detail that is highly necessary for an organized and secure life.

SO YOU'RE DIVORCED . . .   THINK CHART

Thoughts to think

Lists to list

How am I doing?

Books I've always wanted to read

	ROTTEN	BETTER	GREAT
After 3 months			
After 6 months			
After 9 months			
After one year			

People to invite to a party

Things to do for others

What to do when I'm in the dumps?

What do I like about myself?

Hobbies

Am I getting into bad habits?

Is it time yet to stop pampering myself?

My blessings

SO YOU'RE DIVORCED . . .   THINK CHART

Chapter Two

YOUR NAME AND ADDRESS

||||C3|||||||||||::C3|||||::|||||C3||||||||||||C3|||||||||||C3||||||||||||C3|||||||||||C3|||||||||||C3|||||||||||C3||||||||||C3|||

At this point you may not yet know *who* you are, but right now is the time to decide about your new name. You have two choices.

Once your divorce is final, you are no longer Mrs. Harold Klutz. Which in a way is a blessing, because you've been half of him long enough. Besides, it's possible he will get himself a new wife, which would make two Mrs. Harold Klutzes floating around. According to etiquette, if you were once Mary Bedford, you are now Mrs. Bedford Klutz. Informally, you are Mary Klutz.

Your second choice is to revert to your maiden name. That's who you were for many years, and that's who you're going to be again. We're not pushing you into this, but we know that many women do it, feeling that one's own name makes one her own person, a definite help in the healing process.

If you've already had it legally changed in the divorce decree, fine. But even if the judge denied your request (possibly because of your children), you can use your maiden name. If you have children, the fact may put a damper on the idea. After all, they carry his name. If they keep it and you change yours, that makes for potential confusion at schools, etc. If you have children in their teens or older, you can talk it over with them to discover how they feel about it. In some cases, kids have been so turned off by their father that they actually welcomed the idea of taking their mother's

21

name themselves . . . a switch that of course requires legal action.

Whichever you choose, you must establish the change of your name in many areas. How do you go about it? Easy . . . by law, it is accomplished by common usage. But you must notify a lot of people to change their records.

If you opt to be Mary Bedford again, notify *all* of the following. If you choose to keep his last name, make this known in any of the areas listed below in which you need to chop off the "Mrs. Harold."

- Make certain your lawyer has made the name change on deeds of any property you now own—property in which your former husband has no vested interest.
- If you have been awarded securities of any kind, such as stocks or bonds which you and your husband formerly owned jointly, your broker will implement the name change for you via a "transfer agent."
- If you now own United States savings bonds, apply to a Federal Reserve bank for a name change. Large city banks have a special window for the business of United States savings bonds.
- Your passport. To obtain a new passport issued in your name only, you must furnish the Passport Office with your old passport, plus evidence via your divorce papers that the court has allowed you legally to change your name. However, there is an easier way. Even if the court has not given you such permission, you may have your existing passport amended with the addition of your new name under A.K.A., which stands for Also Known As. Your passport will then read "Mary Bedford Klutz, A.K.A. Mary Bedford." For this you may apply at any time, but must furnish proof of your divorce (via your papers), plus an ID showing common usage of your new name. Your new driver's license is an acceptable ID in this procedure.

Passports are often dealt with at offices of the United States Postal Service. Check with your nearest post office to learn if they might handle this for you or, if not, to which Passport Office you should apply.

- Notify all utility companies.
- Apply to Social Security for a change of name on their records. Contact the Social Security Administration district office nearest you; they will issue you a new card, and you will retain your old number.
- If you are continuing in the same job, tell your employer you have done away with your married name and ask him to issue your paychecks in the name you were born with.
- Notify the post office and your personal mailman that you'll be receiving mail addressed to a different name.
- Take his name off your mailbox and replace it with yours.
- Have your checking account changed, and checks printed with your name.
- If you have a savings account (we fervently hope so), change that too.
- Advise the telephone company. Ask them to list your name in future with your chosen name and first initial only. *M. Bedford* instead of *Mary Bedford* will eliminate the blatant announcement that you have no man in the house, thereby avoiding both burglars and obscene phone calls.
- Advise all clubs in which you have membership. Don't forget the automobile club.
- Advise publishers of magazines to which you subscribe. It'll take them a while to make the change, but they'll get around to it.
- Advise holders of all insurance policies.
- Library card.
- Credit. This might be a sticky wicket. (See Chapter Three, *Your Finances.*) If any credit manager wants

your married name as well as your birth name, remind him that the federal Equal Credit Opportunity Act makes it legal for an applicant to use any name she wishes unless she intends to defraud. Your honest face should convince him you are not planning to buy a sable coat and flee elsewhere. At any rate, notify issuers of all credit cards and, if you have one, your credit card service bureau.

- Car registration. As is the case with all state agencies, laws vary from state to state. Phone the Department of Motor Vehicles and ask if you can have your name changed, on both registration of your car and your driver's license.

- Voting. The same applies here. Some states allow a change in name registration; others do not. Write your Registrar of Voters to find out.

- Your will. Last, but certainly not least. If you've already made your own will, make sure it is in your name. If you haven't attended to this, you'll find information regarding it in Chapter Three, *Your Finances*.

While on the subject of your name, think about whether you want to *appear* married or single. What about your wedding ring? It's up to you if you want to continue wearing it, but the majority of divorced women are happy to put it away somewhere to be bequeathed to one of their children —or sell it. Some observe the custom of wearing it on the ring finger of the right hand. But if you're going to look ahead and not back, why wear it at all? If by this time your fingers have swollen to the point where you can't remove the ring, a jeweler will remove it from your finger for a nominal charge.

Your Address

What type of home are you living in? House? Apartment? Condominium?

If it's a house, and he hasn't insisted you sell it so he can share in the proceeds, think long and hard before you decide to sell. Granted it holds many unpleasant memories, but with a little ingenuity (see Chapter Five, *Your Home*), you can do away with most of those. The point here is that you should not make any snap decisions when your head isn't screwed on quite straight. This is no time to get involved in the hassle of choosing a new place. Our advice is to stay where you are, if at all possible. Particularly if you have children, who shouldn't undergo too many changes in their lives at one time.

An apartment? The same advice goes, with the exception of the obvious fact that it's easier to move from one apartment to another than from a house. Sit in it and on it for a few months, especially if you plan on getting a new job, until you know what your income will be.

A condominium is the best place to stay planted. Maintenance is taken care of via ownership, plus the fact that it gives you, we hope, a garden or patio. This style of living affords you the most freedom to hurl yourself into new interests as well as a career.

The only valid reason for moving anywhere in a hurry is the expense of your current home. If its maintenance is more than you can afford right now, perhaps a simpler place to live is a good idea. But remember moving costs, which are exorbitant. It's best to wait many months. You can decide then, after you've settled into a job, whether or not you can afford the new place you have your eye on—and whether or not your present home is now too large for your needs.

Should you decide to move for any reason, be sure to read Chapter Eleven, *Your Moving*.

Wherever you live, advise the post office of HIS new address. He may forget to do this himself, or may purposely neglect to do it in order to have an excuse to stop by for his mail. Unless you want him hanging around, make sure his mail is delivered elsewhere.

YOUR NAME AND ADDRESS   DO CHART

ACTION	PRIORITY	DONE	HOW TO
Name Change			
Deeds to property	1		Check with your lawyer
Stock certificates	1		Ask your stockbroker
Bonds	1		Ask your stockbroker
U. S. Savings Bonds	1		Federal Reserve bank
Passport			See text
Utilities	1		By phone
Electricity			
Water			
Gas			
Heating fuel			
Cable TV			
Others			
Social Security	1		Nearest Social Security office
Paycheck	1		Notify employer
Post office	1		Fill out form at P.O.

YOUR NAME AND ADDRESS   DO CHART

ACTION	PRIORITY	DONE	HOW TO
Mailman, mailbox			
Checking account	1		Your bank
New checks printed	1		Your bank
Savings account	1		Bank or Savings & Loan
Telephone	1		Call service representative of telephone com-
			pany
Billing			
Directory listing			In writing
Club memberships			
Auto club			
Private			
Book			
Record			
Others			
Subscriptions			Write subscription department of each maga-
			zine, journal, etc.
Newspaper delivery billing			By phone

YOUR NAME AND ADDRESS — DO CHART

ACTION	PRIORITY	DONE	HOW TO
Holders of insurance policies			
Library card			
Out-of-town friends			
Credit cards	1		Write each firm, giving credit card number
Credit card service bureau	1		By mail
Car registration	1		Phone Department of Motor Vehicles for information
Driver's license	1		Phone Department of Motor Vehicles for information
Voter registration			Write your Registrar of Voters, listed in phone directory under the name of your county
Your will	1		See your lawyer
Change of Address			
Yours	1		Send form supplied by post office to all of the above
His	1		Notify post office of his current address

28

YOUR NAME AND ADDRESS THINK CHART

Thoughts to think

What's my name?

Do I *have* to move?

Do I *want* to move?

Lists to list

Stocks, bonds, etc.

Credit cards

Friends, relatives to notify

Subscriptions

Clubs

YOUR NAME AND ADDRESS   THINK CHART

30

Chapter Three
YOUR FINANCES

It's our collective opinion that you can't—or shouldn't—get on with the business of everyday life until your financial situation is sorted out. Knowing precisely how you stand will leave your mind free for other things, including decision.

For the most thorough advice possible, get a copy of *Sylvia Porter's New Money Book for the 80's* (Doubleday). Without it, or in the interim, here are our own recommendations:

Plant yourself at a desk. List all income you have at present: from job, interest on savings, investment income, child support, plus any alimony. (If you've been awarded alimony, you are lucky. If you're actually collecting it, you're even luckier. Only 14 percent of divorcees are granted alimony and of those, less than half collect it. Which means that roughly 6 percent of you have income from your ex.)

List your current budget, which will be smaller than formerly because you're not feeding him, paying the dry cleaner for his clothes, or the water company for his showers. If there's no money left over when you subtract expenses from regular income—or, worse yet, if you *owe* money—then you must find a way to increase that income. (See Chapter Nine, *Your Work.*)

If possible, pay all immediate debts now. You're on your own to establish a good credit rating.

Monthly Budget

Income	Outgo
Salary	Mortgage or rent
Bonuses	Food
Children's	Fuel
contributions	Phone
Interest	Electricity, gas
Dividends	Water
Alimony	Property tax
Child support	Income tax
Rentals	Health insurance
Notes held	Car insurance
Other	Home insurance
	Life insurance
	Car: gasoline & repair
	Medical, dental
	Dues
	Charities
	Clothing
	Installment payments
	Schools
	Christmas, other gifts
	Child care
	Home repairs
	Trash collection
	Entertainment
	Other
Total amount $	Total amount $

Learn what payments you'll have to make regularly—mortgage, car, loans, insurance on house and car, etc. Get a large yearly calendar and make a note of due dates of all payments for every month. Also, note any payments due you, such as alimony, child support, dividends, etc.

The Bank

If you haven't had your own checking account, start one. Preferably at a bank offering free checking accounts. Investigate the "free" claims; some banks won't charge for processing checks but do charge you for buying the checks. Many offer free checking accounts if you maintain a specified minimum in your account. Some pay interest on money in checking accounts. Increasingly, banks are offering overdraft checking accounts. This means you can write checks for more than the balance in your account—a handy opportunity in emergencies—and the bank will cover for you up to a certain limit. You pay for this, of course, when they sock the interest to you. After all, it's a loan.

HOW TO BALANCE YOUR CHECKBOOK

Hundreds of thousands of women have never balanced a checkbook and, when first faced with the bank's statement chockablock with numbers and dates, throw up their hands in bewilderment. If you're one of these, take heart—it isn't all that difficult.

First of all, you must keep a record of each check you've written—the date, the number of the check, to whom it was written, and the amount, and keep a running balance by subtracting the amount of each check.

Okay, the bank sends you a record of your account according to *their* records. They spell it out by adding to your last month's balance any deposits you have made since—and subtracting the amount of each check they have processed for you. They also note a charge for any services they have rendered, such as the printing of personal checks. It's a vast relief when you figure it out and find your balance agrees with theirs. A comfort, incidentally, also shared by men.

However, the balances will not agree if . . .

(1) The bank has not listed all your deposits to date.

33

(2) Any checks you've written have not cleared through the bank.

(3) You have not deducted service charges made by the bank.

So . . .

(1) Compare your record of deposits with those listed by the bank. Add to their balance figure any deposits they have not listed.

(2) Again comparing their record with your own, cross off every check they have processed. Those that have not yet come through are called outstanding checks. Total these and subtract this sum from the bank's balance.

(3) Subtract from your own record any service charges. *Voila*, you and they should come up with the same balance.

If it all rattles your brains, here's a simple example. Your checkbook shows you have a balance of $60, but the bank's statement says your balance is $70. You find they haven't yet recorded that $10 you deposited yesterday. Add it; their balance should be $80. The only check you have written that hasn't yet cleared is one for $20. Subtract $20 from their balance (as they will when the check shows up) and their balance matches yours at $60.

SAVINGS ACCOUNT

Open a savings account under the name you've chosen for yourself. Opt for a bank that is a member of the Federal Deposit Insurance Corporation, or a savings and loan firm belonging to the Federal Savings & Loan Corporation. In these institutions, your money is insured against losses up to forty thousand dollars per one account in any bank. Savings and loan firms pay higher interest on savings than do banks.

Ask a bank or savings and loan officer about the ways you

can hold a savings account in tandem with your children. There are several ways, some avoiding inheritance tax. While talking to him, let him know you are newly divorced and ask for any information you need. Part of a banker's job is to help people. As one told us, "I'd welcome any woman newly alone and confused to come in and dump-truck her questions onto my desk."

One of these questions might be about the new type of checking account which federal regulations began permitting in 1978. Banks will now transfer money from your savings to your checking account as checks come in. In effect this gives you a checking account that bears interest, because every dollar earns interest until it is transferred. But beware the charges most banks make for this service—the charges may well exceed the interest you earn.

SAFETY DEPOSIT BOX

Get your own safety deposit box. Some savings and loan firms provide one free if you have an account with them. For a list of things you should keep in the safety deposit box, see Chapter Four, *Your Records.*

Credit

Few of you can go through life paying cash for everything you buy. Furthermore, America has come to the ridiculous state in which many merchants view you with suspicion unless you are awash in credit cards.

You'll be wise, therefore, to establish a credit rating under your own name as quickly as possible. As Mrs. Klutz, credit was attributed to your husband; *you* rated zilch, even though you may have paid many of the bills from your own earnings. (If you marry again, you can now open a credit account separate from that of your husband—or jointly in his name *and* yours.)

Time was when a new divorcee applied for a credit card and was turned down flat simply because she was a divorced woman. Things have changed, thanks in part to women's libbers. As we've already written, the federal Equal Credit Opportunity Act allows you to use a name other than your married name. Plus, you can no longer be turned down on the basis of sex, marital status, age, race, color, or religion.

BUT. If you haven't a steady job with a steady paycheck, it can be quite difficult to obtain your first credit card. Evaluators at credit companies get fairly smarmy when asked why they pass or flunk you. Oh yes, they say, they do adhere to the ECO Act and have no bias. No, the fact that you've paid your utility bills under your own name doesn't help. No, they have no suggestions as to how you can establish credit. "Just apply," they say, "and we'll let you know." Some of them deny consulting your file at the credit bureaus —pretty silly, because that's where everybody checks you out. Another thing they don't talk about: creative people with flexible income—women who are artists, writers, musicians, actresses—are automatically assumed by credit firms to have two heads, neither operable. A woman with a steady job as a dishwasher at minimum wage has a better crack at a credit card than a painter whose work hangs in a museum.

Here are a few ways to help you qualify for a credit card.

(1) If you have any securities—stocks or bonds—we hope you've already changed your name on these. If so, you can borrow money from your bank, using the securities as collateral. Say you have five hundred dollars worth of securities. Borrow one hundred dollars from the bank to be paid back in perhaps five installments. This will cost you a small amount of interest but, in paying the bank promptly on your loan, you will have established an excellent credit reference.

(2) Open charge accounts with a few merchants who know you—your service station owner, butcher, pharmacist. After you've paid their bills a few

36

times, *on* time, then you can bend your knee to the credit card companies.

(3) Few people like to do this sort of thing, but if you're really up the creek, ask a solvent, responsible, and good friend to cosign your application.

(4) It will help matters if you can furnish a statement of your net worth to credit firms. This is easy to do and, unless you're drowning in debts, will give you a considerable lift—99 percent of you are richer than you think. You simply list your assets, then your liabilities, subtract the latter from the former, and you have your net worth. Here's a list to help you work it out.

ASSETS

Cash on hand, or anywhere else   _____

Balance in checking account   _____

Balance in savings account   _____

Cash value of life insurance
(amount you can borrow on it)   _____

Current worth of stocks, bonds,
mutual funds   _____

U. S. Savings Bonds   _____

Money available now from profit-
sharing plans, retirement funds,
etc.   _____

Car, current market value   _____

Home, market value; i.e., realistic
selling price   _____

Other real estate, market value   _____

Money owed you by others   _____

Value of furniture, furs, jewelry,
etc. (make it half of what you
estimate)   _____

*Total Assets*_____

LIABILITIES

Owed on home mortgage, total _____

Owed on car, total _____

Taxes payable within a year, for which *you* are responsible _____

Rent payable within a year _____

Unpaid bills, installment debts, etc. _____

*Total Liabilities*_____

NET WORTH_____

If you are refused credit, it is your right to know why. Ask for a written statement giving the reason, plus a condensed version of the information on which the institution based its refusal. It is the law that such a request must be met within sixty days. If the report of a credit bureau was in any way involved, you have the right to examine your personal file in the office of that credit bureau. The Fair Credit Act states, "Every consumer reporting agency shall, upon request and proper identification of any consumer, clearly and accurately disclose to the consumer the nature and substance of all information (except medical) in its files on the consumer at the time of request." The credit bureau must also disclose the source of its information in a consumer report.

Getting a copy will cost you about five dollars, a small fee for the opportunity to discover omissions or mistakes that need correction . . . and you may request same.

If you have no file, it's a good idea to ask the credit bureau to establish one. (TRW is a credit reporting agency with nationwide offices.) Incidentally, these firms recognize your credit rating with utility companies.

If you have a knotty problem getting credit and the state in which you reside has a Department of Consumer Affairs, phone this agency. Tell them your difficulties in concise language and they will refer you to the appropriate office that will investigate for you.

Whatever you go through to get your first credit card, which opens the door to others, it is worth the time and trouble.

There are two distinct *kinds* of credit cards.

There is no charge for the first type, the bank card. You get the card free and start with an average of five hundred dollars monthly credit which, as you prove yourself a good risk, will gradually be raised. Examples of the bank card are Visa and Master Charge. If you can pay only a portion of the monthly bill you will be charged interest on the balance. There is a notice in fine print that this will cost you about 1.5 percent interest. Read on, because it is also explained (by law) that this amounts to 18 percent annually. Therefore, if you charge a thousand dollars a year on this sort of credit card and make only minimum payments, you are throwing $180 out the window. Additionally, you'll be eternally in debt—a condition not recommended for you now, or ever. One of these cards is usually sufficient to handle your regular monthly bills. But beware of the fact that these firms are reputedly slow in posting your payments. Often when you've already paid your bill of, say, four hundred dollars and later present the card for something costing over one hundred dollars, you are turned down by the sales clerk who has phoned to check your available credit. This time lag in posting is a definite nuisance when traveling. Many hotels will not even accept this type of credit card because they cannot be sure of your balance of credit. Some hostelries are so stiff-necked that they refuse your travel agent's voucher instructing the hotel to bill the agent. Instead, they insist you arrange an alternate form of on-the-spot payment.

The second kind of card has unlimited credit and is acceptable everywhere. This is referred to by most people as "a travel and entertainment card"; issuers term them "convenience cards." Examples: Diners Club, Carte

Blanche, American Express. There is never an interest charge, because you must pay the bill in full every month. There is, however, a charge to obtain one, averaging twenty dollars with the same cost billed annually. This type is much harder to obtain, as they are granted only to people with a comparatively high income level. But they are worth having because, with them, your credit is never questioned.

It is advisable to have one credit card of each of these two types. Many of us are prone to stuffing our wallets with a wad of credit cards. The disadvantages of this are (1) there are so many bills every month that you lose track of the debts you are running up, and (2) if you lose the wad, it's that much more hassle to report the loss to each credit firm. Why have a bunch of them when two will suffice?

If you *do* get yourself a batch, consider membership with an organization like the Credit Card Service Bureau of America (P. O. Box 1322, Alexandria, Virginia 22313). For twelve dollars a year, the CCSB gives twenty-four-hour-a-day service in the event of missing credit cards. They will alert every credit card company on your list, arrange for replacements and, if you're in an emergency situation such as traveling, they will wire you a loan of one hundred dollars interest-free for one hundred days. They will even arrange for an airline ticket to get you home.

We suggest you also secure credit from an oil company and, again, keep it down to one or two accounts. A gasoline credit card allows you to fill up the tank when your wallet is slim. Also, if you use your car for business, you will have a record for the IRS (Internal Revenue Service) at the end of the year of the number of gallons you've bought.

You'll want credit accounts with department stores, which specialize in "revolving accounts." This means they hope you'll pay only a small portion of your monthly bill, thereby earning for them a sizable amount via finance charges. Pay in full when you can.

In addition, a supermarket check-cashing card is a handy

thing to have on weekends when banks are closed and you haven't enough cash for groceries.

Do obtain credit cards. They make life easier, tidier—and often help serve as identification, as when you need to cash a check with a stranger.

Their only disadvantage is the temptation to spend money wildly. And you *are* spending money when you sign each sales draft. Try to keep your charges within your budget, pay the bill promptly and—even with a bank card— in full each month.

If you ever get so deeply into debt that you need help, write National Foundation for Consumer Credit, 1819 H Street N.W., Washington, D.C. 20006, for a list of counseling services in your area.

Useful tips about applying for credit—law as of June 1978:

(1) You do not have to list your gender on credit applications, nor do you have to designate Miss, Mrs., or Ms. A lender may ask for such information in granting a loan for building or buying a home, but answering is your option.

(2) You can't be asked your marital status when applying for a credit card, an overdraft checking account, or an unsecured loan for which you don't put up collateral. Under some circumstances, such as application for a mortgage, the lender can ask your marital status but only as "married, unmarried, or separated," with no further details.

(3) A lender can't refuse to include alimony, child support, or separate maintenance payments as part of your income. But you can be asked questions such as number and age of children, cost of their care, obligations for alimony, child support, or maintenance payments.

(4) You can be asked about your ex's income, but only

41

if you are relying on his alimony payments.

(5) Now that you're divorced, you cannot be required to change your account, reapply for credit, or change the terms of your existing account, *so long as you are willing to continue being liable for your account*. Even if your husband's income was included in support of *your* credit, you can't be asked to reapply.

(6) If you find you are being discriminated against in applying for credit, know that you have the right to sue for damages. This awareness gives you valuable leverage in your credit dealings.

Taxes

PROPERTY TAX

If you now own any real estate—your home, other buildings, or land— you'll have property tax to pay. Look into all of these now so that you can include the payments in your annual budget.

The following states have complicated laws concerning community property: California, Washington, Arizona, Idaho, Louisiana, Texas, Nevada and New Mexico. Even though a marriage has been dissolved, the "community" angle can still exist, resulting in a tax bill mailed to a divorcee. So if you live in any of these states, check out with the county tax collector's office any property you owned in tandem with your husband.

Be sure to claim your homeowner's deduction each year; this amounts to considerable saving. If you are sixty-two or over, investigate tax relief for the elderly.

INCOME TAX

Income tax is a formidable subject for women whose husbands have dealt with the chore as well as the bite. Those federal and state booklets sent you in the mail are as easy to comprehend as a Chinese newspaper. The sensible solution is to employ the services of a good tax accountant or CPA. If your former husband had this sort of help, it might be advisable to use the same man or firm, as they have records of the years during your marriage.

Be careful in choosing your tax consultant. Ask your banker, ask knowledgable friends for their recommendations. If you work, your employer might recommend his own tax consultant. Ask all candidates if they are members of the National Association of Tax Consultors, and avoid those who are not.

Be prepared for the whammy laid on single people. At this writing, singles are taxed at a significantly higher rate than married people. No, it isn't fair, and it's being worked on in Washington, but in the interim you've joined the club of singles who groan at the inequity.

If you have children living with you, be sure to claim "single head of household," which will save you a sizable chunk. If you work, you can deduct the expense of child care. You should keep *complete* records of money you spend on the kids—their clothes, food, percentage of housing, even car expenses (after all, you chauffeur them all over town all year long). Because if you provide more than half of a child's support, you can claim that child as a deduction. (Such records are invaluable in the event their father decides *he* is going to claim them as a deduction.)

Money you receive for child support is not taxable, nor is a lump-sum property settlement, nor a fixed sum to be paid you in less than ten years. But any money you receive on a regular and continuing basis, as alimony, *is* taxable. If you are one of the rare women who pay alimony to a husband, you can list him as a dependent and deduct the current dependent allowance.

Don't take our word for anything having to do with taxes, as tax laws change constantly. Just get yourself a good tax consultant and use the above information as a guide when talking with him.

To learn what you should keep for possible IRS questioning, as well as your report to your tax consultant, see Chapter Four, *Your Records.*

Securities, Investments

As we've advised in the chapter *Your Name and Address,* if you own stocks, bonds, property, or United States savings bonds, make certain these assets are now recorded under your own name. It is highly important that these name changes be made immediately. As we've pointed out, once you have such assets in your own name, you can borrow money using them as collateral, thereby establishing your own credit.

If you want to invest any money from here on in, professional help is most definitely needed. As with other specialty services, check with friends and business associates to find yourself an investment counselor and/or a real estate broker who you feel is right for you. It is a good idea to talk personally with three people in each field before you decide on one. It might be less time and trouble, and more rewarding, for you to pick a name from a membership list of the Investment Counsel Association of America, Inc., whose address is 127 East 59 Street, New York, New York 10022. A stamped and self-addressed envelope along with your note will bring you a list of members as well as a gratis book explaining investment counseling. Remember that these people will charge you for their expertise.

It is a sound idea to invest. Money left in a bank or savings and loan is eroded by inflation, as well as diminished through income tax paid on interest. If it just sits there, you're losing money. A good investment counselor can help your money make more money.

You should keep careful records of all investment; this will be outlined for you in Chapter Four, *Your Records.*

Social Security

We assume you have a card. If you haven't, and qualify for one, apply at the nearest Social Security office, listed in the phone directory under United States Government.

Social Security records of your earnings are kept according to past W-2 forms, plus reports from your employers. The records are not always complete; therefore it is wise to ask periodically for their compilation. A checkup every three years is best because, unless you can furnish proof of earnings within the past three years, Social Security will not change its records. If you find they have omitted any earnings, you can request that these be added to their records.

If you were married for twenty years or more to the same man, you can claim his Social Security benefits in lieu of your own. This, of course, is advisable only if his income exceeded yours. It's the only possible bright spot for a divorced woman in the matter of Social Security. As a single, your benefits will be much less than those given a man married to a woman who perhaps has never worked. It's an irritating fact but it's there, in company with your income tax bite as a single person.

Social Security does not notify you when you are eligible to collect retirement benefits; you must contact them. You don't have to wait until you're sixty-five; if you opt to take benefits at age sixty-two, you will be paid 80 percent of your full benefit. Contact them several months before the date you wish the payments to commence.

Insurance

Here again, you need professional help. The average insurance salesman sells policies only for his own company. We therefore suggest that you find an independent agent. You might try a woman; female agents are comparatively new in the field, but that doesn't mean they're any less qualified. In many cases, women who sell insurance are more likely to understand the needs of other women, whether or not children are involved. If you can afford it and deem the cost worth it, hire an insurance *consultant*. These people offer knowledge of a wide scope of policies and insurance companies. You can get a list of insurance consultants, free, by sending a stamped, self-addressed envelope (business size) to Society of Insurance and Risk Management Consultants, 835 Glenside Avenue, Wyncote, Pennsylvania 19095. What is *not* free is the cost of the advice, which runs from twenty dollars to as high as one hundred dollars an hour.

LIFE INSURANCE

Do you need it? Only if there is someone you wish to provide for after your death. Elderly parents and young children are the sensible beneficiaries. Life insurance has been with us so long that many people buy policies and pay into them all their lives without thinking about the *need*. If you have grown children they are probably on their own, in which case it seems ridiculous—unless you want to provide college expenses for them—to pay premiums for their benefit. If you have no family, you definitely do not need life insurance.

Roughly, there are two kinds. The first is term, which gives the highest protection and has the cheapest premiums. The second is whole or straight life (the two words are used interchangeably). The latter is a forced savings policy, as it accumulates a cash value. But think before you buy; if you yourself save the money you would otherwise pay as premiums, plus any additional savings you achieve, you will effect the same goal—cash for your dependents after you're gone. And your savings will be drawing interest to boot.

So *think* about life insurance.

HEALTH INSURANCE

You definitely need health insurance. If you were covered in the past under your husband's policy, whether his was included in his job benefits or he arranged for it independently, you are no longer covered.

46

If you have a job and your benefits include membership in a group health plan, read the policy, including the fine print. Check your nearest hospital to learn the daily cost of care, and then decide if your present coverage is sufficient. A hospital bill can wipe out savings within a few weeks. It's a very good idea to supplement health insurance that covers you in a group plan by buying a second policy on your own.

If you are not covered via a job, arrange for health insurance immediately, and if you can afford it buy policies with two different companies.

Few women are covered by disability insurance, but in today's world where women constitute over 40 percent of the nation's working force, women need it just as much as men. Health insurance may pay the hospital, the doctor, the surgeon—but if you're sick, who's going to pay the rent, the utility bills, the cost of food for the children? Disability insurance is highly expensive, but well worthwhile if you can afford it.

See more about health insurance at the end of Chapter Seven, *Your Health*.

CAR INSURANCE

Now that the car is in your name, you are responsible. Car insurance should not only cover the cost of straightening fenders but protect you against damage suits brought against you as a result of accident. There'll be a deductible on car repairs, of course, but the main need for car insurance is coverage for injuries to others. Most insurance agents recommend Bodily Injury coverage of $25,000/$50,000; Property Damage, a minimum of $10,000; protection against uninsured motorists, $5,000. The deductible for collision insurance now runs about two hundred dollars, the deductible for Comprehensive, fifty dollars. Like all insurance, it is expensive, but it may cheer you to know that women between the ages of twenty-five and forty-five (if the kids don't drive) are charged the lowest premiums.

If you need further cheer, it is a statistical fact that, and

47

we quote, "a middle-aged woman driving alone in mid-afternoon is the safest driver on the road."

HOMEOWNERS INSURANCE

Fire, of course, is the first thought relating to the insurance of a home. Inflation has driven up the cost of replacement to an enormous increase over the original cost of building, and premiums have increased accordingly.

But if you own a house, you need insurance. There are policies for fire damage only, but it's wise to buy a homeowner's policy that covers you not only for fire, but also for theft, damage by wind or water, loss of personal property, and medical payments to those who may suffer injury while on your property. If you live in an apartment, there are Homeowner's Tenant policies; these cover the contents of your apartment, provide money for living expenses in the event of "loss of use," and liability to others. The amount of fire insurance should be figured according to the cost of replacement and, in the case of a house, coverage is necessarily high. If it's covered by a policy arranged for by your ex, check this to learn if coverage matches today's replacement cost. And notify the insurance company if the house is now in your name.

An absolute minimum of twenty-five thousand dollars is par for fire insurance on a house. Personal liability is also sold at a minimum of twenty-five thousand dollars coverage, but the premiums for this are quite low. And worth it, because you never know when a houseguest is going to crash through the shower door and decide to sue you.

Borrowing Money

Do *not* go to a loan shark. A loan company without a state license in all probability deserves the name of "shark"—and this is an outfit that can pitch you into a tangle of debt.

If you do need to borrow money for any reason—and it had best be a good reason—you can borrow against a life insurance policy, safely and at comparatively low cost. If you have securities as collateral, as we've already told you, you can borrow easily from a bank. If you work, you might get an advance against your salary.

Whatever your source, be certain you know the *annual* rate of interest charged, which is required by law to be stated. Don't confuse it with the daily or monthly interest.

If you have an overdraft checking account and don't need much more than five hundred dollars, you can obtain the money at your bank.

Lastly, there are your friends and relatives. But this is the fastest way to lose a friend, so think twice. And if you do borrow from a friend, insist on paying the current rate of interest.

The best solution is not to borrow at all . . . "Neither a borrower nor a lender be."

Perhaps you can *barter* with a friend or acquaintance. If your need is a roof repair or an overhaul of your car and you have a talent of your own, it's possible you can trade new shingles or carburetor for a set of lessons in Spanish or a needlepoint pillow you've made for the repairman's wife. This sort of thing is being done increasingly; in many cities there are organizations that cross-file applicants. In Santa Monica, California, Knowledge Exchange (P.O. Box 3336) will register you and charge you only $2.50 each time they find a barter partner for you.

Your Will

Many people neglect making a will, shunning the thought that they are going to nip off at some time in the future. Like it or not, we all are, and there's no worse mess than leaving family and friends in a quandary about your wishes.

Do them a favor and get cracking with this. You're on your own now, and it is your responsibility. You may want to try to save money making a holographic will (one executed in your own handwriting), but we strongly advise that you employ legal services instead. If you insist on bypassing your lawyer and making a will on your own, do it with advice that can be trusted. An excellent book on the subject is recommended at the end of this chapter. But given the chance, your lawyer will draw up the document in airtight fashion, and probably for a lower fee than you've imagined. He should keep the original, to be immediately available to your heirs, and you should have a copy to put in your safety deposit box.

Appoint an executor you trust, and who you figure will outlive you. And make a note to check your will in another year or so. It's quite possible that in your current emotional state you might make decisions you will later want to change.

While on the subject of leaving this world, you should write a "letter of instruction" regarding funeral arrangements. We'll take up the matter in the following chapter, *Your Records*.

Recommended Reading

Sylvia Porter's New Money Book for the 80's (Doubleday).

The Seven Laws of Money by Michael Phillips (Random House, paperback, $3.95). A book that restructures your attitudes about money. Practical tips teaching you how to use money rather than let it use you.

The Only Investment Guide You'll Ever Need by Andrew Tobias (Bantam, paperback, $2.50). Enjoyable reading for even the most sophisticated investor.

Consumer Reports (Annual) Buying Guide (Consumers Union/Consumer Reports Books, paperback, $3.00). Published each December and dated for the following year. Evaluation of almost every major purchase—indispensable guidance for the consumer.

The Joy of Money by Paula Nelson (Stein and Day, hardcover, $7.95). Guide to women's financial freedom.

Consumer's Buying Guide (via Better Business Bureau,

paperback, $1.50). Valuable information on buying almost anything.

How to Write Your Own Will by Harper Hamilton (Hamilton Press, 4720 Hancock Drive, Boulder, Colorado 80303, paperback, $6.95). A trial lawyer, Hamilton has written the most explicit book available on holographic wills.

YOUR FINANCES

DO CHART

ACTION	PRIORITY	DONE	HOW TO
Buy a book about money			See text
Make out your budget	1		
Pay all debts now due	1		
Note regular payments to be made—and received	1		Make complete record on monthly pages of calendar
Start your checking account	1		
Have checks printed in your name	1		
Open a savings account	1		Bank or savings and loan
Get a safety deposit box	1		Savings and loan (free?) or bank
Get credit cards in your name			See text
Limited credit ("bank")	1		
No credit limit ("convenience")	1		
Gasoline company	1		
Department stores	1		

YOUR FINANCES   DO CHART

ACTION	PRIORITY	DONE	HOW TO
Credit Card Service Bureau			See text
Supermarket check-cashing card			See text
Figure your net worth			
Learn property taxes (Are they included in your mortgage payments?)	1		If records aren't located, contact your county tax collector
Claim homeowner's deduction, if you qualify	1		Contact county tax collector
If sixty-two or over, learn if you qualify for property tax relief	1		Contact county tax collector, or senior citizens group
Decide who will be your tax consultant	1		See text
Check out your Social Security benefit records	1		Nearest Social Security office
Notify Social Security three months prior to initiation of benefits	1		
Make a record of your former husband's Social Security number if you were married twenty-plus years	1		Check with his tax consultant

53

YOUR FINANCES

DO CHART

ACTION	PRIORITY	DONE	HOW TO
Arrange for life insurance—*if* you need it			See text
Arrange for health insurance	1		See text
Get car insurance in your name	1		See text
Arrange for homeowner's insurance	1		See text
If homeowner's insurance exists, (1) check if coverage is sufficient; (2) notify insurer home is now in your name	1		See text
Make your will	1		See text, and consult your lawyer

YOUR FINANCES

THINK CHART

How much more money per month do I need?

How can I cut down on expenses?

Chapter Four
YOUR RECORDS

This is a paper world, and you may as well face the fact. Very little of the mountain of paper in a lifetime is important, but the things that *are* important must be kept safely. The safety deposit boxes offered free to savers by some savings and loan firms are small, but should be adequate unless you have a cache of valuables to stow away— in which case you can rent a larger box for under fifteen dollars annually.

Keep in Safety Deposit Box

Birth certificate, marriage certificate, divorce papers, adoption papers.

Passport.

Ownership certificate for your car.

All deeds, titles, and mortgages having to do with property.

Copy of your will. (Original with your lawyer.)

Stock and bond certificates.

Copy of life insurance policy. (Original should be kept at home because some state laws require that safety deposit boxes be sealed for some time after the owner's death.)

A copy of your Social Security card.

Business contracts.

A list of your valuables at home—jewelry, furs, antiques, etc., including the cost or worth of each. In case of loss, the value will be most satisfactorily proved to a claims agent if you've had a professional appraisal made, plus color photographs of each item.

The safety deposit box is primarily for those things of value to which you seldom refer. However, there are items in everyone's life that are irreplaceable but should be kept at hand. We therefore advise that you locate a duplicating machine such as a Xerox copier in your neighborhood, a convenience you'll be using often. Make copies of the following to be kept at home, and put the originals in your safety deposit box.

A list of your credit cards, their numbers, and the phone number for reporting loss of each.

A list of the serial numbers of your car, TV, radio, stereo, cameras, tape recorders, etc. Copies will be available at home for police in case of theft.

A complete record of all securities—the name of the stock or bond, number of shares, price paid, date bought, date sold, and price received. These must be kept up to date for the IRS.

The final thing to keep in both your safety deposit box and at home is a letter of instruction to be read after your death. We seem to leave last things last but, as we've said on the subject of your will, such preparation is true courtesy to your family and friends. The letter of instruction is a sort of supplement to your will. In it you write the location of all your important papers (insurance, will, securities, savings, investments, etc.), the name and address of your attorney and, if you have decided, the funeral arrangements you desire. If you don't put the last in writing—well, you just might end up next to *him* for all eternity.

Keep in Your Desk

A list of the things you've stored in the safety deposit box. This will save both your time and nervous system because you won't have to look endlessly for something, having forgotten it's stowed in your miniature safe.

Your copies of lists of credit cards and serial numbers.

Original of life insurance policy.

A file containing warranties and operating instructions for all your appliances.

Record of every dollar you spend on the kids, if their support is wholly or partially the responsibility of your former husband. Don't be shy; include everything—care and feeding, cost of chauffering, etc.

Records pertaining to income tax. Keeping these is a bore, granted, but much better than being nicked by the IRS for insufficient proof of deductions. For a small sum you can buy a cardboard box in which to keep canceled checks. Retain everything relative to costs that may be deducted; your tax consultant will tell you what these are. In a separate place, perhaps a large envelope, keep a record of your previous tax returns and of your earnings during the year, including W-2 forms. Keep records of all medical expenses, contributions to charity, and sales slips for expensive items to prove sales tax deductions. If you own a house, keep records of all improvement costs, which will be deducted from your profit if the house is sold. If you have business expenses, keep bills for travel cost, plus entertainment both at home and in public places. Should you use one or more rooms in your home as your place of work, keep records of phone and utility bills, rent or mortgage and upkeep expenses, etc. A percentage of these costs (equal to the percentage of the daily time during which the space is used for business) can be deducted from your earnings by your tax consultant. It is essential that you keep meticulous records; the IRS frequently challenges these deductions.

How long do you keep all this stuff? The IRS gives out a bit of gobbledygook on the subject . . . they say three years. But if they suspect fraud and turn inquisitive they can back up farther than that. So play it a bit safer and keep records for the past five years, especially if there's been a sale of property, investments, anything important that requires proof positive.

On Top of Your Desk

That calendar we keep talking about. If you mark it with obligations due—and this includes things such as birthday cards to friends as well as the mortgage payment—the desk calendar is going to keep your life functioning smoothly.

Recommended Reading

Personal Records: The New York Times Book of Lifetime History by Margaret Ann Mardon (Times Books, $12.50). Gives spaces for everything from your birth certificate to your will.

YOUR RECORDS

DO CHART

ACTION	PRIORITY	DONE	HOW TO
Get desk calendar with large page for each month	1		
Locate duplicating machine, such as a Xerox copier	1		Savings and loan, bank, post office
Obtain a safety deposit box	1		
Put in the safety deposit box	1		
Birth certificate			
Marriage certificate			
Divorce papers			
Adoption papers			
Passport			
Auto registration			
Property deeds, titles, mortgages			
Copy of your will			Copy to be kept in car
			Original will be kept by your lawyer
Letter of Instruction			See text
Stock and bond certificates			
Record of securities bought and/or sold			
Health insurance policy			See text

YOUR RECORDS

DO CHART

ACTION	PRIORITY	DONE	HOW TO
Car insurance policy			
Homeowner's insurance policy			
Copy of life insurance policy			
Copy of Social Security card			
Business contracts			
List of valuables at home			Original to be kept at home
			See text re necessity of appraisal and pictures

Appraisal
Picture
_____

Appraisal
Picture
_____

Appraisal
Picture
_____

YOUR RECORDS

DO CHART

ACTION	PRIORITY	DONE	HOW TO
Appraisal Picture			
Appraisal Picture			
Appraisal Picture			
Appraisal Picture			
List of all credit cards and their numbers			
List of serial numbers Car			

DO CHART

ACTION	PRIORITY	DONE	HOW TO
TV			
Camera			
Radio			
Stereo			
Tape recorder			
Other			
Keep in your desk	1		
Copy of credit card and serial number information (for police in case of theft or loss)			
Copy of securities bought and/or sold			
Copy of Letter of Instruction			
Original of life insurance policy			
File of warranties and operating instructions for appliances			
A list of everything in your safety deposit box			
Start a notebook for recording expenses for the children			

YOUR RECORDS   DO CHARTS

ACTION	PRIORITY	DONE	HOW TO
Start a file for the IRS	1		See text
Box for canceled checks			
File for sales slips, car expenses, medical costs, business expenses			
File for expense of house repairs and improvements			
File for income tax data of previous years			
Record of income during current year			
Record of charitable contributions			

YOUR RECORDS   THINK CHART

Chapter Five

YOUR HOME

It's *your* home now, and unless you want him coming to visit whenever he's in the mood, make certain he has taken everything that is his—clothes, books, guns, records, pictures . . . anything he can use as an excuse to drop by. Once his things are out of there, have your locks changed on all doors. Have an extra set of keys made; you no longer have his keys as a backup if you lock yourself out. Find a new hiding place for the "extras"—if both of you used to stick them in the potted geranium, that's the first place he'll look.

He's not the only one you need protection from. It may be your castle now, but there's no moat around it. So the first subject we tackle pertaining to your home is:

Your Safety

Don't pinch pennies when choosing locks. In addition to the regular lock, each door should have a deadbolt lock made of steel or brass. This means you must open both locks whenever you come home, but the cost and trouble are well worth this security. Patio doors, particularly the sliding glass type, are a cinch for burglars. If your home has these you can get advice in a free booklet called "Home Security Starts at Your Door" from Consumers Information Center, Pueblo, Colorado 81009.

If you are a nervous Nellie about living alone, the same source will send you, free, a pamphlet titled "Home Security

Alarms." Burglar alarms cost a bundle, but if you feel you need one and can afford it, give yourself that peace of mind. (And *use* the warning stickers supplied.)

If you live in an apartment, install a chain lock and, if possible, a peephole.

Don't forget to lock up at night. It might have been his chore in the past; now it's your responsibility.

Advise your landlord (if you have one), the local police, and friendly neighbors that you now live alone.

If your area has a Neighborhood Watch (wherein members keep an eye on adjacent houses), join it, by all means.

If you have a garden, install floodlights and keep them lit if you expect to return home at dark.

A garage door opener is a wise investment. Your headlights will illuminate the whole garage before you drive in.

If you must put out trash for collection, do it during daylight hours.

Your mailbox should display only your last name, and perhaps your first initial.

If a stranger telephones you, do not reveal your name or address. If someone claims he has reached a wrong number, don't give him yours, but ask what number he wanted to dial.

We strongly advise that you do not keep a gun in your home. Too often an intruder will use such a weapon on you.

In the event of a power shortage you'll be grateful for a battery-operated radio. Also candles and matches. Keep a candle (in a candlestick) near your bed, another in the kitchen.

Make sure you have an operable flashlight and remember where you keep it. (If you ever beam a flashlight from a window into the garden or driveway, it's highly advisable not to stand directly behind it. This would make you a bulls-eye target.)

Here's a tip in the event you should suspect the presence of a prowler outside your home. Next time you entertain a group of friends, tape their conversation. When played on your recorder, this will forthwith discourage a burglar from trying to enter your home.

What do you do if you are alone and hear someone else in the house? Phone for help immediately. If you're in bed and the room is dark, you can dial "Operator"; if you have light, dial the three-digit number that summons help in your area. Memorize this number. In the rare event an intruder has removed a second phone from its hook, go to the nearest window, throw it open, and yell, "FIRE!" A call for help is often ignored by fainthearted neighbors but the subject of fire involves them, too, and anyone within earshot will be there in seconds.

Suppose you come home and have reason to suspect that an intruder is in your house? (Lights showing differently from the way you left them—or a strange car, more likely a truck, in the driveway.) Do not go in to find out. Take the license number of any vehicle unfamiliar to you. Then go to a neighbor's home and call police on their phone. Stay there until arrival of the police . . . who would prefer a false alarm to missing an opportunity to catch a thief.

If you are a dog lover, have a dog. The barking is a definite deterrent to burglars.

FIRE PROTECTION

Every home should have a hand-held fire extinguisher, the type that puts out electrical and chemical fires as well as burning wood, etc. Read the instructions; you won't have time to do that after you discover a fire. If you have need to use it, remember to point the extinguisher at the *base* of the flames. These hand-held extinguishers should be inspected every year to make certain the pressure remains sufficient.

Smoke detectors are fine warning systems and have not only improved in recent years but are lower in price and less obtrusive than when they were initially introduced. Firemen recommend the battery-operated type as opposed to those powered by electricity. Many fires *are* electric and if your power is out, an electrical smoke detector will not work.

Firemen also recommend use of a warning device called, in most areas, "tot stickers." When adhered to a left corner of a window, these act as a signal to firemen that there is a child in that particular room . . . or someone ill or elderly. If your fire department doesn't have a supply of tot stickers on hand, they'll tell you where to get them.

If you live in a two-story house, a rope ladder may save lives. These are made specifically for escape in case of fire.

If you have children, put them through a fire drill periodically, until they learn well enough to respond automatically in the right way.

When You Go Away

- The safest place to hide valuables is in the attic; burglars don't like to go any place where they can easily be trapped. Do *not* hide valuables in the master bedroom; this is the first room they ransack. They know all about such hiding places as the refrigerator and behind books; about things taped beneath the lid of the toilet tank or to the underside of furniture. Keep all small valuables in your safety deposit box. Above all, don't leave a lot of cash in your home.
- Disconnect your TV set. Chances are slight, but if you neglect to do this and there's an electrical storm, you may return to find your home burned to a crisp.
- Automatic timers for radio and lights are a good investment against theft while you are absent from home. The light that burns all night, every night, serves only as a tip-off that no one is home. So set a couple of lights for varying times that coincide with average "awake" hours.
- Have newspaper, milk, and other deliveries discontinued while you're away.

- Leave a door key with trusted neighbors in case of emergency, and ask them to pick up throwaway papers and package deliveries.
- Instruct the post office to forward or hold your mail.
- In summer, arrange to have the lawn mowed.
- Cover the phone with a pillow. An accomplice can call your home and, if the burglar nearby hears your phone ringing, unanswered, he is sure the house is vacant.
- At the last minute before you leave, make sure the heat or air-conditioning is turned off, that nothing is lighted in or on the stove, that all windows are locked (except perhaps an open window or two upstairs, which makes the house appear occupied as as well as supplying fresh air). And that all doors are locked. *Double* locked, we hope.

A postscript about possible burglary. At home or away, you take less chance of being ripped off if you have etched your name or driver's license number on the sort of valuables thieves tend to steal—appliances, cameras, typewriters, etc. This is easier done than you might think; burglary ID kits are available for less than ten dollars at hardware stores, and it's a simple process anyone can do. It effects a definite deterrent to burglars, who prefer not to steal identifiable items.

The Telephone

We've already advised you to have only your first initial listed in the directory.

Tape emergency numbers to all phones—fire department, doctor, hospital, police. Have the kids memorize these.

Think about that second phone. Do you need it?

Concerning long distance calls, familiarize yourself with the cheaper rates. All telephone directories list these varying rates. Calls cost less if made between 5:00 P.M. and 11:00 P.M.—and lowest of all if you call on Saturdays, Sundays until 5 :00 P.M., holidays, or between 11:00 P.M. and 8:00 A.M. If you live in the East, for instance, you can call West Coast friends a bit after 11:00 P.M. your time, which is 8:00 P.M. their time. If you're on the West Coast, get up early and phone your eastern friends during their midmorning (7:30 A.M. in the West is 10:30 A.M. in the East).

Do you need an answering machine? These are worth their weight in gold, particularly if you have a business in your home. When you tape your message, do *not* say, "I am away for three days" or any similar tip for potential burglars. Instead say, "I'm not able to come to the phone. Please leave your name and number, and I'll call you back as soon as I can."

The Obscene Call

How can you handle obscene phone calls? Hang up immediately and then leave your phone off the hook for about ten minutes. What they want from you is reaction, and if you don't offer this, they probably will not call again. Some women handle obscene phone calls with a dash of humor, a sure squelch for the caller. We know of one woman who said, "Look, I'm expecting an important business call, so if this is an obscene call, snap it up." Another, a proper Pasadenan, was horrified after she hung up to realize she had said in reply to a vulgar question, "No thank you, but thank you for calling."

If a caller persists, contact the Information operator and ask the phone company for help. In any case, don't be afraid of attack by these wacks; according to psychiatrists, they are inhibited and fear being caught.

Hot Line Help

The federal government has set up a number of bureaus to help citizens with various problems. Many of these are unnecessary to you now, but if you ever need help in any of these areas you can call toll-free (except from Alaska and Hawaii).

- For evaluation of the safety of products, or reports of injuries caused by faulty products, call the Consumer Product Safety Commission: (800) 638-2666.
- For housing problems dealing with discrimination, call the Fair Housing and Equal Opportunity Hotline: (800) 424-8590.
- For information on installation of solar heating and cooling, call the National Solar Heating and Cooling Information Center: (800) 523-2929.
- If you have a new car that is definitely faulty in operation, or if your car has been recalled by the manufacturer, you can phone National Highway Traffic Safety Administration: (800) 424-9393.
- If you plan an extensive trip by car within the United States, you can obtain travel information and a map of U.S. highways by calling Travel Hotline: (800) 323-4180.
- Help will be given if you plan moving your household goods to another state, or have a complaint against a moving company that has treated you unfairly. Call Interstate Commerce Commission: (800) 424-9312.
- If you're interested in an educational grant for your children, information is available at: (800) 638-6700.
- If your teenager has run away, advice is given by the National Runaway Switchboard (twenty-four-hour service): (800) 621-4000.
- If you're interested in the Peace Corps, Vista, or a similar service, call Action: (800) 424-8580.
- If you live in a flood area and would like flood insurance sponsored by the government, call National Flood Insurance: (800) 424-8872.
- If you live in a high crime area, you can buy govern-

ment insurance. Call Federal Crime Insurance:
(800) 638-8780.

Costs

Most of the questions regarding cost of your home have
been answered in Chapter Three, *Your Finances,* but here
are a few extra tips:

Check your mortgage and find out if the mortgage company includes property taxes in your payments, in which
case *they* pay the tax collector.

If your mortgage payments are too hot to handle right now,
consider refinancing your house to secure lower monthly
payments.

Try living with 68° in winter and 78° in summer. Adjust
the thermostat.

Also adjust the thermostat on the electric blanket for your
own comfort. If you have a dual control, you can save a
bit by turning his side off.

Adjust the hot-water heater control for less consumption.
And try setting its thermostat ten degrees lower. Unless
you're expecting a baby, who needs *boiling* water?

If you need money, think about renting part of your
garage as storage space for someone who needs it.

A great deal of money can be saved through insulation.
Attic insulation alone can save 20 percent in heating and
cooling costs. Check with your fuel company for information.
Check to see if you have weather stripping on windows and
doors. For those of you who are do-it-yourselfers, see the
advice on insulation given later in this chapter under "Repairs."

Maintenance

In winter, unless you live in a subtropical area, you'll
need snow removal service. Don't try shoveling the white
stuff yourself; your back and heart are just as likely to go

out as a man's. (For emergencies, however, learn now where he last left the snow shovel.)

In the summer, there's the garden. If you need help, check your local high school, which probably has a list of kids wanting to earn money on weekends. If you are elderly, you might contact the local Senior Citizens Center and ask them to find help for you. Regardless of who does the gardening, a variety of tools is needed. A suggested list: shovel, hoe, cultivator, rake, hand cultivator, pruning shears, a hose and nozzle. Get one of the newer-type nozzles featuring a hand control for on and off; this saves you tearing to the water bib to turn off the water at its source when the phone rings.

You'll need help in the installation and removal of storm windows. Maybe that high school boy?

When freezing weather threatens, you can prevent frozen pipes if you turn off the outside water lines . . . *if* they are controlled separately from the inside water supply. Ask the meter reader next time he comes by and ask him, too, the location of the master turn-off valves, in case of emergency.

Learn, too, how to turn off gas lines and electricity. Both should be shut off in the event of earthquake. Your gas company will cooperate in showing you how, as will the power company serving you. In the fuse box there is a master switch that, when thrown, turns off all electricity to the house. The smaller switches or buttons control separate sets of wires in your house. When lights won't work, this usually means either a blown fuse or a circuit breaker that needs resetting. Buy several fuses to keep on hand, and learn how to install them.

If your house has gutters and downspouts, remember that by November of each year these are filled with dead leaves and are unable to function properly in the runoff of rainwater. Also, the weight of the collected water will often cause damage to the roof from which the gutters are suspended. Air-conditioners, too, often get clogged with leaves and should be kept free of debris. Find yourself an all-

74

around helper for chores like these. If you want to do it yourself, keep in mind that ladders may look harmless but a lot of spinal injuries are the result of falls from ladders. Always make sure a ladder is set firmly on the ground before you climb it. If you want to get on your roof, lean the ladder at an angle of at least forty-five degrees so that it won't fall backward with your weight.

Have an annual check made of your furnace, boiler, or other type of heating equipment. It may need a new filter, a cleaning, or simple repair, but the yearly checkup should prevent a major repair that would probably take place only after you had shivered for several hours or days.

If you are lucky enough to have a swimming pool, employ pool service only if you have no teenagers in your family. We think if they can enjoy the pool, they're big enough to keep it clean.

Don't let the house go too long without a fresh coat of paint. The longer you wait the more expensive the job will be, because old paint will need to be sanded off. If you see paint beginning to flake, it's time for a new coat.

Repairs

Women in overalls no longer look odd; we're now installing pipes and climbing phone poles. Few repairs around a home need the strength of a man.

You'll need tools, so line them up in a handy place. A hammer, preferably one with a claw that is used to remove nails. A regular screw driver. Also a Phillips screwdriver; instead of a flat end (−), the Phillips screwdriver head has four niches along the sides and is used on screws fashioned with a cross (+) in the head. A hand saw. Nails of assorted sizes. An awl, which is much like the old ice pick and is used to punch holes prior to insertion of screws. A pair of pliers, indispensable. A monkey wrench, which can be adjusted to grab things of various sizes, including stubborn tops of pickle jars. A plunger, in case a toilet becomes clogged. There's something called plumber's putty, used for small leaks in pipes. If you keep a small can on hand it may save you a bill, or at the very least stem the leak until a plumber arrives. You should have a caulking gun (which works as simply as squeezing a tube of toothpaste) and caulking, to seam cracks around the tub, or around doors and windows.

The first time you meet up with an electrician, ask him to show you how to replace a fuse and reset a circuit breaker.

First time you meet up with a plumber, ask him how to replace a worn-out washer. Washers are those little rubber circular things in the ends of hoses and inside faucets.

If the toilet flush decides not to work, (1) try jiggling the handle; (2) lift the "float bulb" and replace it; if it doesn't sit where it's supposed to, it doesn't shut off water from the intake pipe; (3) check the tank ball to make sure it plops squarely on top of the hole at the bottom of the tank; (4) if you haven't fixed it by now, you'll have a plumbing bill.

When the garbage disposal gives up, don't call a plumber until you've tried "the red button." There's one on every garbage disposal, usually on the bottom, and many times if you merely push this button the disposal will return to normal.

We advise that you revert to helplessness if you find a pilot light is out. Gas is nothing to fool around with, nor is propane. Too many eyebrows have been singed, or worse, by people who don't understand combustibles. Phone your gas company for help.

If you want to save a great deal of money by insulating your house yourself, it isn't all that hard to do. A bit messy, but not difficult. Use your caulking gun on cracks appearing between unlike materials, such as plaster and wood. Weather stripping around doors and windows is really a simple job; ask your hardware dealer what material he recommends—

felt stripping, foam rubber, whatever—and the type of nails you need.

The attic is a major problem in loss of heat. Insulating it is tax deductible (as of this writing), so make a note to advise your tax consultant. If your attic space is uncluttered by beams, you're lucky because you can buy insulating material in "blankets" and simply unroll these between the long timbers. If the attic is full of small spaces, you need "batts" of insulating material and a sharp knife to cut the batts to fit. You'll also need time and patience, but it can be done. If you're not the type to crawl around an attic, hire a contractor, either to do the above work or to blow in stuff called cellulose fiber from the outside. Get three estimates from listings in the Yellow Pages under Insulation Contractors. Before deciding on one, check with the Better Business Bureau to learn if customers have lodged complaints against any of the three firms. (In point of fact, this sort of checking up on any local company whose help you plan to hire is a sound idea when you're faced with faulty wiring, a leaking roof, wet basement, cracks in the foundation . . . any of the hassles frequently dumped on homeowners.)

We strongly recommend that you buy a book on the subject of home repairs. You'll find suggestions under "Recommended Reading" at the end of this chapter.

Enjoy *Your Home*

Now in particular, you want a home you love to come home to. If it holds depressing memories in the form of inanimate objects, get rid of these. Is his favorite chair sitting there staring at you? Include it in a garage sale, or give it away.

Does the front door bother you? It's surprising how many divorced women have felt this way, reminded always of the evenings he came home from work. Well, paint it a different color, or cover it with wallpaper.

Change the whole house, to *your* personality. Rearrange furniture, hang some new plants. Change the bedroom in particular. You can make it over to your taste now. Fill it with pillows, hang more feminine curtains. Put your stereo in the bedroom, and a TV. Buy a simple bookcase and fill it with the kind of books you like to read before going to sleep. Make the bedroom your favorite room in the house.

Clean out the closets, and while at it get rid of any clothes related to your departed mate. Dresses he liked that you didn't, perhaps gifts from him you never really cared for. Clean out the attic and the garage. This sort of activity is a psychological catharsis and will result in a pile of things for a super garage sale. Ask neighbors to join the venture. It's more fun that way, and it removes the idea of a "divorce sale."

Plant an herb garden. Herbs are not only the answer to a gourmet's prayer, they are lovely to look at and waft a delightful fragrance.

Get some new pets. If he hated poodles, now you can have a poodle. Or a bird—even a goldfish or two.

Who says only men can build a good fire? The secret is *space* between materials. Stuff strips of "wrung" newspapers under the grate. On top, sprinkle lightweight kindling wood; crisscross it, leaving space between. On top of that, a couple of small logs. Once the fire has caught, toss on the big logs. Nothing will make your home cozier on a winter evening than a crackling fire. Just remember *never* to go to bed while it's still burning. This requires a bit of planning; don't add new wood for some hours before bedtime. Your fire department will tell you the *only* way to be sure is to douse it with water. This creates smoke, but once you get the hang of it, said smoke should go up the chimney where it belongs. But here we've put the horse behind the cart . . . smoke will go up a chimney only if the flue is open. The flue handle is inside the fireplace, above the opening and in the center. You'll have to stick your head in there and look up when you move the handle to learn which direction opens the passage.

Finally, dine like a lady, not like a truck driver at Joe's Eats. Unless pressed for time, don't eat at the kitchen table or, worse, standing up at the counter. Set a place at the regular dining table, and set it nicely. Keep flowers or fruit or a plant on the table. Use a wine glass, not an old jelly glass. Light candles. Believe us, this sort of thing will make your meal more enjoyable and will add to your self-respect. We knew of a divorced woman whose mother told her before she died, "Joan, I'm leaving you all my crystal and silver. Promise me you'll use and enjoy it." For the last dozen years, Joan has dined every night, with guests or alone, at a beautifully set table. Even the condiments are in their silver containers. She told us, "The habit has made my life infinitely more pleasant."

Maybe you don't have Haviland china or Waterford crystal, but do use your best things and enjoy them. If you have children, this habit will grace their upbringing—for which favor they should darn well wash the dishes.

You may be alone, but you have a lot of company all over America. So many people are living alone these days that manufacturers have hopped into the marketplace with mini-teakettles for one, single-hamburger cookers, even a single-hot-dog steamer—and Campbell has a whole line of Soup for One.

Recommended Reading

Superwoman by Shirley Conran (Crown Publishers, hardcover, $8.95). A bestseller in England, this book is a joy for any woman; from shortcuts in housecleaning to mastering the metric system.

Toll-Free Digest by Toll-Free Digest Co. (Warner Books, paperbacks, $1.95). Published annually, it lists by topic thousands of useful toll-free phone numbers.

The Unhandy Handyman's Book by George Daniels (Perennial Library paperback, $1.25). For those "who fix things because they have to—whether they know how or not."

Reader's Digest Do-It-Yourself Manual (paperback $17.95). Expensive, but worth it because of complete illustrations.

YOUR HOME

DO CHART

ACTION	PRIORITY	DONE	HOW TO
Make certain he has taken all his belongings			
Have locks changed	1		See text for safety types
Extra keys made			
New hiding place for extra keys			
Burglar alarm installed			
Advise police you live alone	1		
Join Neighborhood Watch			
Install outside floodlights			
Garage door opener			
Battery-operated radio			
Flashlights, spare batteries and bulbs			
Candles and matches			
Near bed			
In kitchen			
Record your next party on a tape			
Buy a fire extinguisher	1		See text re safety use

81

YOUR HOME

DO CHART

ACTION	PRIORITY	DONE	HOW TO
Smoke detector installed	1		See text
Tot stickers on windows	1		See text
Buy a rope ladder			
Start fire drills with kids			
When leaving home overnight			
Remove excess cash to safety deposit box			
Put jewelry in safety deposit box			
Disconnect the TV			See text
Set automatic timers for radio and lights			
Discontinue newspaper			
Leave key with neighbor			
Discontinue milk delivery			
Have mail held by post office			
Cover phone with pillow			
Arrange for mowing of lawn			
Turn off heat, air-conditioning			
Check stove			
Lock windows and doors			

YOUR HOME

DO CHART

ACTION	PRIORITY	DONE	HOW TO
Etch name on valuables			See text
Order new listing in phone directory			First initial only
Tape emergency numbers to phone	1		Check your directory
Teach children all emergency numbers	1		
Have phone extension(s) removed if now un- necessary			
Buy telephone answering device			
Hot line numbers			Check text for any you need
Check mortgage re property taxes inclusion	1		
Adjust heat thermostat			
Adjust hot-water temperature			See dial on hot-water heater
Insulate			See text
Windows, doors			
Attic			
Hire snow removal service			
Hire garden help			
Find a general handyman	1		

83

YOUR HOME

DO CHART

ACTION	PRIORITY	DONE	HOW TO
Garden tools			
Shovel			
Hoe			
Cultivator and hand cultivator			
Rake			
Pruning shears			
Hose			
Hose nozzle			
Learn location of water turnoff	1		Ask water company
Learn location of gas turnoff	1		Ask gas company
Learn operation of fuse box and circuit breakers	1		Ask power company
Buy fuses			
Check gutters and downspouts for debris			
Annual checkup of heating equipment	1		
Annual checkup of air-conditioning			
Pool service			
Check need for paint jobs			

YOUR HOME

DO CHART

ACTION	PRIORITY	DONE	HOW TO
Tools			
Claw hammer			
Screwdriver			
Phillips screwdriver			
Hand saw			
Assorted nails			
Awl			
Pliers			
Monkey wrench			
Plunger			
Plumber's putty			
Caulking gun and caulking			
Snow shovel			
Learn how to replace washers			Ask your plumber
Buy a book on home repairs	1		See text for recommendations
Rearrange furniture			
Clean closets			
Garage sale			See hints under Chapter Eleven, *Your Moving*

YOUR HOME

THINK CHART

Chapter Six

YOUR CAR

You are in the driver's seat now, both figuratively and literally.

The first thing that disturbs divorced women about driving is that they are doing it *alone*. Perhaps for the first time since the wedding, they drive alone at night. For the safety of all of you, follow these rules, especially when it's dark.

- Never get into your car without checking the back seat and floor to make sure no one is there. At night this requires a flashlight; keep one under the driver's seat.
- Check your gas gauge before leaving home. Never allow the tank to be less than a quarter full (and *never* carry spare gasoline in your car). Here's a small lecture on checking the gas mileage of your car; if you know this you're a lot less likely ever to run out of gas. Your average miles-per-gallon ratio is easily arrived at by dividing the number of miles you've driven since the last fill-up by the number of gallons you buy. Keep a record of the mileage each time you fill the tank or, if your car has an adjustable mileage gauge, turn it to 00000 every time your tank is filled and you'll always have a record of miles driven. You'll note a considerable difference between city driving and highway driving. Always figure the lower number of miles per gallon your car gives. Rather safe than sorry.

- If your garage hasn't an automatically opened door, lock it when you leave home.
- Try to avoid parking lots that insist you leave your keys. If you must patronize one, leave only the ignition key, never keys to your home or any identification giving your address.
- When approaching your car in a self-parking lot, always have your key in hand. And try to park in a lighted area.
- When driving, keep doors and windows locked. If you need air, turn on your blower and/or open windows about one inch, never wide enough to allow space for a hand to enter.
- When stopped for a traffic light or stop sign, always keep your car in gear, ready to go. If you are approached by a stranger you think is menacing, lean on the horn and take off.
- If you think you are being followed, do not drive to your home. Ideally, drive straight to a police station, a maneuver guaranteed to lose your follower. Or into an open service station.
- Lock your car when you leave it. Eighty percent of stolen cars have been left unlocked—and 42 percent have had keys left in the ignition.
- Keep valuables in the trunk, never within sight of anyone passing the parked car.
- If you have mechanical trouble while driving, pull over and stop. Raise the hood of your car, then attach something white—a piece of paper, or tear your slip if you have to—to the raised antenna of your car. This is a distress signal noted by police cars. Then sit inside with doors and windows locked until police help arrives.
- When you come home at night, keep your headlights turned on until you have opened the garage door, driven your car in, and unlocked the door of your house.

- Never, never pick up a hitchhiker. Steel your heart against lone girls waving a thumb; an accomplice may be hidden nearby. It isn't easy to turn down some of these people, but police advise that you do. They use clever ruses; one of our contributors picked up a girl holding a baby in a receiving blanket. The "baby" turned out to be a doll, and the "mother" forced the driver at knife point to hand over her purse.

- Remember that the only person who can legally force you to stop your car is a policeman. If you are involved in an accident you're required by law to stop and give the other driver information about your insurance. Do this from inside your car, with the window down only an inch, enough to allow your voice to carry. Would-be assailants often *cause* minor accidents with a lone woman driver to entice her out of her car.

- Should your gas pedal stick, pump it a few times. If this fails to make the pedal operative, shift into neutral, pull over to the side of the road, and turn off the ignition.

- You no longer have a second car as a backup, so check your local transportation facilities. You may need to use them if your car refuses to start and you're in a rush.

- Have you membership in your own name with an auto club? This is a must for you; the service and safety are well worth the annual bill. Keep one membership card in your wallet, a duplicate in the glove compartment. (If the glove compartment is equipped with a lock, *keep* it locked.) And, is the next renewal date marked on your calendar?

- Have you an extra set of keys? You no longer can borrow his. Don't leave them in the car—keep them in the house.

- Is the car now registered in your name?
- The certificate of ownership should be in your safety deposit box.
- The registration card should be kept in the vehicle at all times, at hand for presentation to a peace officer on demand.
- If your state or local law requires periodic inspection, learn when and where this should be done. Note dates on your calendar.
- When should the license plates be renewed? Will the notice be sent you automatically? If not, note the date on your calendar.
- If you've moved, have you notified the Department of Motor Vehicles of your new address? They will update all records: *you* are responsible for changing your driver's license. Cross out the old address, substitute the new, and date and initial the change.
- What are your payments, and when due? Note on the monthly calendar.
- Keep the membership card of your insurance company in the glove compartment.
- Have you the proper insurance? See "Car Insurance" in Chapter Three, *Your Finances.*

Safety of the Car

Your car carries all you love—your children, your friends, and yourself—and should be maintained in top condition. Women, and some men too, assume that a car will "just keep running." Untrue. Maintenance is highly important.

- Look in the glove compartment for the manufacturer's manual and learn how often you should have the car serviced, and for what. If you can't find the manual, get one from your dealer's service department.

- If possible, use the warranty services of the dealer from whom the car was purchased. He will have the proper parts, as well as mechanics who are experts in working on your make of car.
- If you have a used car and no warranty from a dealer, locate an expert mechanic by asking friends, neighbors, coworkers. Or use your friendly neighborhood service station, *if* it is dependable as well as friendly. Ask if they furnish a "loaner" while your car is being serviced.
- For any major repairs, get three estimates.
- Learn how often the car needs a lube job and oil change. Mechanics note these, with dates, on a sticker usually placed on the frame of the driver's door.
- Learn about antifreeze, when it's needed or must be changed.
- Learn proper tire pressure and have it maintained. Include the spare tire. More people forget about this and when they need their spare, find it flat as a pancake.
- Where is the jack? If you learn how to use it, changing a tire is relatively easy.
- If your lights (headlights, tail lights, backup lights) or turn signals don't work, have repair made immediately.

THE SERVICE STATION

Establish a good relationship with the owner of a service station in your neighborhood; during gas shortages you'll be grateful for such a friend. Ask him what is the lowest quality of gas you can use safely and thereby save cost. Lead-free? Low octane? Ask what weight oil your car needs in various temperatures.

Increasingly across America, service stations are giving instruction to women in how to use the gasoline pumps, how to check tires, oil, water, and batteries. Learn these do-it-yourself maneuvers, which will save considerable money in the cost of gasoline. Until you do, have a full checkup made by the attendant *every* time you buy gas.

Be certain your service station makes periodic checks of the fluid levels for your brakes, transmission, and power steering; also the condition of the sundry hoses. A leak in a hose can strand you suddenly. Neglect of transmission fluid can result in a whopper of a bill for a new transmission. If brake fluid disappears, you simply are unable to stop. And without power steering, you can't steer.

Note the condition of your windshield wipers. When they begin to wear out, the resultant murky window can be dangerous on a rainy night. Have the service station install new ones. You can check the level of water for the windshield wipers yourself—it's under the hood in a plastic container that looks like a water jug, which it is. Keep it full via your garden hose.

REPAIRS

Keep all repair bills. If your car is used for business, a good portion of these are tax deductible, as is gasoline used on business trips.

CARRY IN YOUR CAR

First aid kit

Flashlight, with spare bulb and batteries

Two jumper cables (one for your car, one for the source)

Flares (ask your service station)

Aerosol can for tire inflation

White cloth for distress signal

If your climate includes a rigorous winter, an ice scraper, sand, and salt. Keep sand and salt in the trunk —the weight gives added traction.

Fuses (ask your mechanic how to install these)

A "screamer"—a small cylindrical tube with a button that, when pressed, will make an unholy racket that can be heard for a mile. It's a definite deterrent to anyone trying to attack you.

BITS AND PIECES ABOUT YOUR CAR

Wash it yourself, or have the kids do it. One big tip: If you use a vacuum cleaner on the inside, do *not* stand in any pools of water left over from the wash job. Many people have been electrocuted this way.

Before you have the car waxed, check the owner's manual. Some cars have a new style of paint that should never be waxed.

If there's a tear in the upholstery, repair it or have it repaired as soon as possible. These molehills quickly grow into mountains.

Clean out the glove compartment. Make sure the registration card is in there, and keep a map of your city as well as surrounding towns. (If he used to drive this car and you find any surprises in the form of another woman's belongings, by this time you shouldn't care.)

Buying a Car

How to tell you about buying a new one? Advice is important because (1) unless you're in the habit of buying platinum and rubies, the outlay for a new car is second only to that for a house, and (2) the purchase of a car, new or used, is full of pitfalls. In a highly competitive business, salesmen invent countless ploys to lure you into signing a contract.

The subject is much too complicated to delve into here. We suggest you get a copy of *Consumer's Buying Guide*, put out under the aegis of the Better Business Bureau. Or— as for anything dealing with money—*Sylvia Porter's New Money Book for the 80's.*

If you haven't time to dig this deeply, we'll give you a few basic hints.

93

1. Decide exactly how much money you can afford.

2. Ask friends, and read a few of the magazines that deal exclusively with cars. In the spring of each year Consumer Reports puts out an *Annual Roundup for New Car Buying*, available at newsstands and libraries. Decide the make of car you want.

3. Know what you want—a station wagon, a two-door, a sports job. Do you *need* air-conditioning, whitewall tires, power brakes, etc.?

4. Get recommendations of reputable dealers. Stick to those closest to your home, an advantage when you take the car in for servicing under its warranty.

5. *Shop.* Don't sign anything with any dealer until you've investigated prices and the amount they'll allow you on a trade-in for your old car. Note the "sticker price" on every car, and don't pay one cent more than is recommended by the manufacturer.

6. Let time go by, while the various salesmen cool their heels. You can bet if they haven't given you their best possible offer that they'll phone you within a couple of days with a lower price. (This goes for a used car, too.)

7. Shop at the right time of year. Because of depreciation, you're better off buying a car model when it first comes on the market *if* you plan to keep it only a couple of years. If you're going to drive it forever, the very best time of year to shop is August and September, when dealers are trying to get rid of the prior models before the new ones arrive. You can really strike a better bargain at this time.

8. If you trade in your old car on the new one, know that the dealer subtracts at least one hundred dollars from the amount you should get, for his private profit. You can save this by selling the old car on your own, but think about the cost of advertising and the time involved in doing so.

The easiest way in the world to get a lemon is to purchase a used car. To minimize the risks, note the following.

1. Even the *dealer* can't distinguish a lemon from a peach unless he knows the previous (and original) owner.

2. Choose the dealer with care; check his reputation.

3. Avoid buying in summer, when so many people are looking for a cheap car to drive on vacation.

4. If you find what you want, the price seems right (check the *Blue Book* value of used cars, available from the auto loan officer at your bank), and there are no obvious signs the car has been damaged in an accident —test drive it. Drive in heavy traffic, up a few hills, and along a straight stretch, preferably a freeway.

5. Pay your mechanic to test vital parts of the car.

6. Check the tires for wear.

7. If the brake pedal shows signs of wear and the odometer reads less than 20,000 miles, you can bet the odometer has been set back.

Buying a used car is a jungle without much light; you could be lucky or unlucky. Don't take our minimal advice as final. Do read—*study*—*Sylvia Porter's New Money Book for the 80's.* Or *Consumer Reports Guide to Used Cars,* available in paperback for $5.50.

Other Recommended Reading

Auto Repair for Dummies by Deanna Sclar (McGraw-Hill, paperback, $7.95). How a "dummy" can get smart about her car.

Women on Wheels (published by Chrysler Corp., Box 970A-GH, Detroit, Michigan 48203). A free booklet with information on car maintenance, plus tips on driving in rain and snow.

Emergency Repairs (also free, from Dick Hall, Shell Oil

Company, P.O. Box 61609, Houston, Texas 77208. Ask for booklet No. 13). If you prefer not to get your hands dirty, this booklet gives good tips regardless . . . as in "I turn the key and nothing happens, so what do I do?" Or, "My engine turns over, so why won't the car start?" Supplies you with "back talk" in the event you're forced to accept help from a rip-off artist.

How to Deal with Motor Vehicle Emergencies (a free pamphlet from Consumer Information Center, Pueblo, Colorado 81003).

YOUR CAR

DO CHART

ACTION	PRIORITY	DONE	HOW TO
Learn personal safety rules	1		See text
Notebook for mileage record in glove compartment			
Join auto club	1		
Get extra set of keys	1		Key maker or car dealer
Check public transporation			
Legal aspects			
Car registered in my name	1		To change, contact DMV (Department of Motor Vehicles)
Ownership certificate in safety deposit box	1		
Registration card in glove compartment	1		
Note periodic inspection dates	1		Learn when due and where
Check renewal date of driver's license	1		
Check renewal date of license plates	1		
Notify DMV of address change	1		
Note car payments on calendar	1		

YOUR CAR

DO CHART

ACTION	PRIORITY	DONE	HOW TO
Get proper insurance	1		See text
Insurance membership card in glove compartment	1		
Safety of car			
Locate car manual			New one available from dealer
Find a recommended mechanic	1		
Learn service recommendations: lube & oil change, brakes, etc.	1		
Antifreeze	1		
Learn proper tire pressure	1		
Inflate spare tire	1		
Need for snow tires			
Locate tire jack			
Learn to operate gas pump, check oil, etc.			
Have fluid levels checked			Service station
Have hoses checked			Service station or mechanic
Inspect windshield wipers			

YOUR CAR

DO CHART

ACTION	PRIORITY	DONE	HOW TO
Carry in car			
First aid kit	1		
Flashlight & spare batteries			
Two jumper cables			
Flares			
Aerosol can for tire inflation			Service station
White cloth for distress signal			Auto supply store
Ice scraper			
Sand			
Salt			
Fuses			See text. Get at hardware store
A "screamer"			See text
Buying a car			

YOUR CAR

THINK CHART

100

Chapter Seven

YOUR HEALTH

Recovery from fatigue involving nerves takes infinitely longer than that caused by physical labor. Digging a ditch all day needs only one night's sleep. Recovery from divorce requires many months of rest.

This book, it occurs to us, isn't giving you much rest if you are gung ho to do everything at once. Don't let it pressure you. If you spend only an hour a day . . . perhaps three if you're not employed . . . you'll be surprised how rapidly you accomplish peace of mind, because you're steadily banishing all these niggling details.

The point is that you need plenty of sleep. Your body will tell you how much. Just don't fight it; if you've slept a solid eight hours and then feel the need for an afternoon nap, take the nap. Don't feel guilty about laziness, because you're not being lazy; you're regaining your health and stamina.

As we said, divorce is surgery, and following the upheaval you need the same sort of care as would be prescribed after a siege in the operating room. It takes about the same time; in three months you should begin feeling your physical self again.

If you are an average newly divorced woman, you couldn't care less about food. You don't feel like eating, and you certainly aren't interested in cooking. Well, eat . . .and *cook*. If you're lonely at meals, you can chase away the blues by putting your nose in a book or watching television.

If you like to cook, it can be therapy. (Bette Davis has said that whenever her life was in a snarl she cooked up a storm and gave the neighbors whatever food she couldn't freeze for the future.) If you hate to cook, do it anyway. The absolute worst thing you can do to yourself right now is to eat frozen packaged foods and junk food. It's lots cheaper, better, and more pleasant to fix a piece of sole with butter (and maybe cook it with white wine and seedless grapes) than to chomp on Mrs. Snodgrass's frozen fish sticks. We suspect you're skipping breakfast and/or lunch, and tend to nibble through the afternoon on stuff that has no nutritional value. Evening comes, you're not hungry, you eat a hot dog or, if you're starving, send out for pizza.

Right now, your body needs all the help it can get, and the above nonsense is not the way to do it. You *know* better; you learned about balanced diet in school. Don't worry about your appetite; just eat nutritious food when you do eat.

Increase your protein: milk, eggs, cheese, fish, fowl, meat. Be sure to have a vegetable and fruit at least once a day. Eat whole-grain bread for roughage. Be sure to supplement your diet with B vitamin pills. Take a multiple vitamin with *minerals.* You need vitamin C when you're under stress; take one to three tablets of 500 mg. each of vitamin C every day.

You may not be into health foods, but we recommend that you buy wheat germ and eat it with cereal or mix it with yogurt. Wheat germ is inexpensive and loaded with protein and B vitamins.

Instead of keeping the coffeepot on the burner all day, cut out the caffeine—and the tannic acid in tea. Try herb teas, bought at health food stores. Try peppermint or camomile tea. Both are delicious, and refreshing waker-uppers in the morning.

Don't pamper yourself with sweets. Pampering isn't the word for it . . . sugar is addictive. The more you eat the more you want, and right now is no time to begin turning your body into a balloon. You have enough to worry about without discovering you can't close the zippers on your clothes. Forego candy and desserts, and try honey instead of sugar in your herb tea (or coffee, if you must).

Another habit you should avoid is the sleeping pill. Okay, you need it, but give in only occasionally. Valium is the most popular drug these days, and doctors prescribe it rather freely. But some people have been hooked on Valium, with distressing side effects. Try to keep all "calm-down" pills to a minimum; a good way is to take half a pill at a time.

Along with other bad habits, watch your intake of alcohol if you're inclined to cocktails before dinner. You may not be an alcoholic by nature, but the happy hour is habit-forming. If you find yourself drinking frequently or increasing your intake each day, it's time to take a hard look at your dependence on liquor. If you admit it is becoming habitual you would be wise to send for a free booklet that spells out symptoms of the illness of alcohol abuse, how and where to get treatment . . . all of it based on the particular problems of women. Write: Alcohol Abuse and Women, Dept. GH-K, Box 2345, Rockville, Maryland 20852. And remember, if you're on medication, don't drink.

Keep your body trim and firm with exercise. The simplest is a daily walk, which has the added benefit of clearing the mind. (Take your dog with you, a way of meeting new people. For some reason, dog walkers always seem to strike up conversations with other dog walkers.) Positively the greatest thing in the morning, once you've been up for a while before breakfast, is jumping rope. This is excellent for your heart, gets the blood circulating freely and, followed by a shower, makes a morning look beautiful even when it's raining outside. You can buy a jump rope for a few dollars and its benefits will keep you from depression and save you a bundle in doctors' bills.

If you're the type who *believes* in exercise, map out a morning regimen. Evening is better if you work all day;

self-discipline is required to exercise when you are tired, but you get the maximum benefit if you work out when you're dragging your tail feathers. Exercise before bedtime also gives the benefit of solid sleep. A fifteen-minute routine followed by a leisurely hot bath is a combination almost guaranteed to cure insomnia.

Here is a group of exercises beneficial to a woman of any age. If you're out of shape, begin easily, doing each one only a couple of times a day, then build up to ten times for each. (If you have any history of physical problems, call or visit your doctor for approval to begin exercising. And if you feel weak or dizzy at any time, stop exercising and go more slowly the next time.)

1. Reach for the ceiling, then bend forward as far as you can. The simple "toe toucher"—and if you do it often enough you'll soon be touching the floor with the palms of your hands.

2. Raise your right arm, bending it over your head. Now
lean to the left as far as you can, sliding your left arm down
your left leg. Once you're down there, pull lower a couple
of times. You'll feel the muscles straining all the way down
your right side—excellent for the waistline. Do this on the
opposite side, same number of times.

3. Stand with feet together; then raise one knee as high as possible toward your chin. Clasp your shin with both arms and hug your leg to your body. Alternate legs. A good back stretcher and good for the thighs.

4. With feet twelve inches apart and back erect, extend arms to the sides at shoulder height. Revolve them in small circles, both clockwise and counterclockwise, gradually making bigger circles. Good for bust line, plus circulation.

5.   Knee bends are the best possible exercise for the thighs.
Stand near a counter or table in case you need support as
you lower yourself by bending your knees. Keep your back
erect as you raise and lower yourself. Do this very slowly,
both on the way down and the way up It will hurt a bit at
first, proving your thighs need it, so start off with only a
few, increasing each day.

6. So far we haven't put you on the floor, but if you want to firm and tone stomach muscles, the floor's the best place to do it. Lie on your back. Raise each leg, keeping it as straight as possible, as far as you can. Lower slowly. When you've done this one regularly for a week, follow by raising both legs simultaneously. Again, lower them slowly. (If you have a troublesome back, support it during this exercise by placing the palms of your hands on the floor beneath the small of your back.)

7. Jump rope (on a rug if there are neighbors downstairs). If at first it's difficult with both feet simultaneously, start by alternating left and right feet with each rope swing. If jumping rope bores you (and we hope not) then jog in place for one minute.

If you do these exercises, followed in the morning by your shower or at night by a warm bath, you'll agree with us they're the Lucky Seven. The whole set should take no more than fifteen minutes . . . ten, after you're into the routine; and as always, accompanying music will lend enchantment.

All of the seven exercises are done alone. If you prefer company and opportunity to meet new people, join a health club, or check out programs at your local YWCA.

Another method of helping you sleep is relaxation via meditation. You don't need a guru to teach you how. Just sit comfortably and close your eyes, relaxing all muscles. Try to "sink" into whatever you're sitting on. Inhale through your nose, and each time you exhale say the word "one." If you are unfamiliar with meditation this might sound silly, but if you try it you'll find you've shed stressful feelings. This is because it lowers your blood pressure, the rate of pulse, oxygen consumption, and metabolic rate.

Your Doctor

If you have one in whom you have faith, fine. If on the other hand you have no family physician and want to find one, we suggest you look for a woman doctor. Not that her skill is any better than a man's but, because she is female, she understands the problems of other women. She may not do a better appendectomy, but you can bet she'll have the ability to go deeper than your surface symptoms. She understands women's pressures, problems with children, and if she's gone through divorce herself, will be well acquainted with your stress signals.

Whichever, do find a doctor. You should have a complete physical examination at this time, including a comprehensive blood screen which reveals not only blood count, etc., but the level of iron, potassium, and other minerals necessary to your health. A Pap smear and breast exam might also be advisable.

How do you choose a doctor? His or her medical school isn't all that important; what you need to know about education is the residency training. This lasts from two to more than five years, and the best residencies are in hospitals affiliated with medical schools. The longer a doctor has spent in a residency program, the better he's likely to perform. He is a better bet if he holds an appointment to a hospital affiliated with a medical school, and if he is Board Certified. You are within your rights as a patient to ask a doctor these questions. You don't need to ask his age, but it's recommended that he be under fifty, as younger physicians are more likely to keep up with improvements in medicine and surgery. This is not a fast rule by any means, but true in general.

You are also within your rights to discuss fees with his receptionist before treatment.

Don't wait until you are ill . . . decide on a doctor *now*, and have your physical. If you've neglected to do this and need a doctor in an emergency, don't look in the Yellow Pages; go to the emergency room of a hospital. And, with an eye to future safety, keep your doctor's phone number taped to your phone.

If you are getting on in years and/or have a health problem such as high blood pressure or heart disease, you'd be wise to have a relative or friend phone you each day. This sort of daily check has saved many lives.

Also for older women, be advised that Medicare will not begin automatically when you are sixty-five. You must notify Social Security three months in advance of your sixty-fifth birthday in order to get the Medicare ball rolling.

Regardless of your age, you should have in your home a book on first aid. Over half of all accidents happen in the home, and a handy reference for tourniquet application, sunstroke, etc., is indispensable. The first aid book is especially important, of course, if you have children living with you.

Lastly, and certainly not the least important, is your

health insurance. By all means, invest in the policy that gives you the best and most coverage you can afford. Shop for it. Shop well and hard, and be sure you understand the benefits; some of the best known health plans carry the most expensive premiums, yet services do not exceed those in cheaper plans.

As far as we're concerned, you can't arrange for this fast enough; it is most urgent. You may feel well today but tomorrow, God forbid, you may be involved in a traffic accident.

Recommended Reading

Woman's Body: An Owner's Manual by The Diagram Group (Bantam Books, paperback, $2.75). Tells you everything you should know about the magnificent machine that is your body.

Child's Body (Same publisher, same price). Invaluable for mothers.

Take Care of Yourself: A Consumer's Guide to Medical Care by Donald Vickery and James Fries (Addison-Wesley, paperback, $5.95). So good it's like having a doctor in the house.

The Working Woman's Body Book by Lilian Rowen with Barbara Winkler (Rawson, paperback, $4.95). A book of exercises, health, and energy for the working woman, with a thirteen-minute daily program.

YOUR HEALTH

DO CHART

ACTION	PRIORITY	DONE	HOW TO
Exercise regularly	1		See text
Find a doctor	1		See text
Have a complete physical exam	1		
Note date on calendar for next checkup			
If living alone, arrange for daily phone contact with a friend			
For Medicare, notify Social Security if you're approaching sixty-five	1		See text
First aid book to keep at home	1		
Health insurance	1		See Chapter Three, *Your Finances*

114

YOUR HEALTH

THINK CHART

Chapter Eight
YOUR CHILDREN

Handling the situation with the kids can be a blockbuster. That statement is a common feeling of divorced mothers, who fret endlessly over the problem. But according to sociologists and psychologists, there shouldn't be that much of a problem. Their studies show children of divorced parents to be ultimately much better adjusted, more self-sufficient, and less involved in juvenile delinquency than kids who live with both parents in the midst of strife. So stop worrying about it.

There is today an enigma in society's attitude toward divorce. Time was when it was hush-hush, when a divorced woman was often ostracized from polite society, and in those times it was no wonder the kids went through a trauma. But now, with every third (or second?) wedding ending in a split, children of divorced parents have plenty of company among their peers. The enigma is this: While divorce is now accepted as the intelligent solution to a bad marriage, *and* it's been proved that the average child does not incur ineradicable scars, somehow the stigma refuses to leave the minds of divorced women, who subconsciously retain a sense, however small, of shame. Along with this, they worry unduly about their children's suffering. If you feel this way you'd better confront it and correct it. Make yourself trust the fact that your children are better off now than they would have been in a house filled with hostility, whether of the screaming-fight variety or of the unspoken kind that fills the atmosphere with tension. Kids absorb and respond to the attitudes of those important to them. If you communicate, however silently, to your children that your divorce is destructive to them, they will tend to believe it.

Your attitude is your main strength in dealing with the situation.

It is a tender situation that needs careful handling. If you have custody of the children, as is most frequently the case, then they no longer have a father in residence; whether they say they love him or swear they hate him, they naturally miss his presence, usually with considerable pain. Most children don't understand—can't understand—*why* the rift has taken place, and they experience a deep sense of abandonment. Many feel guilty, thinking that the divorce is their fault, that if they'd been better children, perhaps Mom and Dad would still be together. And it is not unusual for a child to tell Mom that he hates her for sending Daddy away. These are the main reactions you have to deal with.

If Dad has custody of the kids and the two of you are on speaking terms, it couldn't hurt to suggest that you discuss our advice with him. And this would certainly be the sensible thing to do if joint custody has been awarded by the courts.

You can't control the father's actions and attitudes when the children are with him, but you can control your own. Answer their questions as honestly, confidently, and cheerfully as possible. Never slough off a question regarding the divorce itself, or their future, however trivial it may seem to you. Emphasize that whatever has gone wrong between you and your husband, *both* of you love the kids just as much as you ever did, and there will never be any change in your love for them. It is the quality of your maternal care, not quantity, that counts. One hour spent with them in every sense is better than "just being there" all day. If you are a working mother, don't dwell on guilt about your absence; just concentrate on the quality of your care.

And don't forget the comforting reassurance, for you as

well as for them, of loving closeness: while you talk, put your arms around them, or holds hands, or simply touch. The point here is love. If they *know* you love them, that reassurance can help to dispel their sense of loneliness. Maybe their father isn't around any more, but this is still their home and you are there and you love them as much as always.

Perhaps most important, let them talk out their feelings if they can; *encourage* this if they are having difficulty expressing themselves. If you truly listen, you'll learn much about their reaction not only to the divorce, but to you and to him.

Fill the gap left by Dad's absence as best you can with other people. Uncles, grandparents, cousins, friends. Retaining a sense of family and normalcy is extremely important.

Never put their father down . . . to the children or within their hearing. He is their father, they have as much right to him as they have to you, and they should never be put in a position of having to choose sides. Encourage the pleasant memories of him. If you grouse and grumble about how undependable he is, how lazy, stingy, sloppy, mean, whatever, they may become defensive about him and champion him at your expense. Or, worse, they may assume any time you're angry with them that you dislike them for the same reasons you disliked their father and will "divorce" them as you did him.

Don't complain endlessly about your burden in hauling yourself and them through life. "Poor me" talk will make them feel needlessly guilty, and guilt does not promote healthy and loving relationships.

You will *want* to complain. It's a rare divorced mother who hasn't chafed under the responsibilities dumped in her lap. There you are, earning a living, keeping a home together, and on top of it being the only one around to bandage scraped knees, talk to the teacher, wipe runny noses, help with homework, and deal with the bad influence of the kids' newest pal who slouches around your home. In the meantime, *he* is off free and running. It's hard to take, sure, but grump to your friends, not the children.

If you've done all you can to insure that this divorce isn't going to cost your kids needless pain, you shouldn't feel any guilt about it. But if you do retain that guilt, you'll be tempted to spoil them, to do them special favors, give them extra treats. Or perhaps you're in an unspoken war with their father for their affection, so you bribe them for their love by giving them everything they ask for. *Don't do it.* If you are a doormat, they will very likely use that fact to get their own way. Dad's discipline is no longer present, and there will be no discipline if they feel they can walk over you. It will make them absolutely miserable. They need to feel that you are in charge. Further, if they are ruling the roost, you are likely to resent them, an unpleasant turn of affections that can be avoided if you make yourself happy.

Remember that you are making a new life for yourself. Be considerate of yourself as well as of the kids; give yourself an occasional new dress, an occasional night out. They'll feel better if you feel better.

And enlist their help with family cares. Without any martyred aspect, explain to them that you are alone in this now, that you need and will appreciate their assistance. Involve them in the business of keeping your home together. If Tommy has a newspaper route, ask him to contribute part of his earnings to the family budget. The same with Fran's income from baby-sitting. Amy may want a new dress for the prom; maybe she can make it herself, with your help. Is the car leaking oil? Bill may know more about cars than you think, along with other repairs he may have watched his father make. Ask him. You may learn that you have a mechanic in the house.

A strong sense of family is fostered by regular meetings. Discuss problems with the children. Here is your income, there is your outlay; how can you all increase the former and lessen the latter? The electric bill was too high last month; will they please remember to turn off the lights when they leave a room and stop opening the refrigerator door every six minutes? Everyone cleans his own room; and who's best at what? Fran does the dishes, Tommy mops the kitchen floor, Amy waters the lawn, Bill cuts the grass. The sharing of chores will not only make the kids more of a pleasure to live with, but in future they'll be better husbands and wives.

It may help you to know (it did us) that a poll taken among teenagers showed that those with divorced parents had more understanding of divorce than the teens with married parents. Teens were asked by Gallup if they thought "divorces are too easy to get." Less than half the children of divorce said yes, more than half the offspring of married parents said yes. Also, kids of divorced parents, in contrast to the others, thought that divorced people do "try hard enough to save marriages." So there is hope that they understand more than you think they do.

Continuing with your own hassle if you have children, there is the mighty mountain of cost. And there is the potential of a future rhubarb with the father about child support; therefore, keep records of what you spend for their food, shelter, clothing, medical costs, schooling and lessons, transportation, day care, baby-sitters. Ideally, he should be taking care of both their higher education and their health insurance.

If your children are small and you work, day care will be a considerable item in your budget. Many women have handled this by arranging with other single mothers to trade children. If Beth takes yours into her home during weekdays, you can keep hers on weekends. Or perhaps you have a friend who works at night and your job is a daytime one; you can make a day-and-night switch.

You're in a phase now where you will become aware as never before of other women—the possibilities of their understanding and help. Hanging together, divorced women, especially those with children, can do much to ease each other's burdens. Institute a car pool; three of you can save lots of time—and gas—with such an arrangement. Instead of paying a baby-sitter, trade off the chore with a friend.

As for baby-sitters, if you haven't a pool with other mothers, give thought to the question, "Do I want to use the same sitter we used to have?" Particularly if *he* is now using him or her himself. The last thing you want is a potential tattletale reporting your private life to him.

The same grapevine exists when the children visit with him, but that's entirely out of your hands. The thing you *can* control is your temptation to ask the kids about Daddy. Please don't make spies out of them. Listen to whatever they have to say, and refrain from comment. If you allay your curiosity about him and the way he's living his life now, it will help you to put him out of your mind and concentrate on your own life. Your lack of interest in him is as much a favor to you as it is to the children.

We don't know what sort of visiting rights he has, but if he's one of those fathers who is forever late in picking them up at your home—or tends to start an argument with you at your front door, or even is a no-show—you might insist that *you* take them to him and pick them up. This avoids hurt feelings for the children, plus saving you a lot of chafing while you wait for him.

Some women use the children as weapons: if he's late with his child support they refuse to allow him to see the kids. *Unfair to the children.* It's confusing enough for them to see him only away from home, and they should not be denied an anticipated visit with him.

On the subject of visiting rights, many divorced couples have found it works best for the children's sake if the father has additional time with them on his own, on some sort of regular basis. As an example, he might take your son to a weekly sporting event, and certainly to any father-son activity. Or take your daughter to lunch one day a month, or pick her up at school and take her shopping on preset days. Such dividend adventures take the onus from the cut-and-dried day with Dad and give the kids an added sense of security.

If they seem insecure in any way and truly upset by the divorce, you would do well to talk with their teachers, the school guidance counselor, and leaders of any clubs to which they belong. These people need to understand the reason behind Tommy's moods or personality changes. They *like* children or they wouldn't be involved in their line of work, so they should be able to give the kids, and you, a bit of help. Counselors at school are, of course, experts in childhood behavior, but you will probably not need to go further in the realm of therapy unless it is recommended by the counselor or prescribed by a physician. Psychotherapy is necessary and effective in some cases. To some children, however, it can be upsetting because the mere fact that you suggest it leads them to suspect that you think they are "crazy." Given time and enough parental understanding to adjust on their own, your children may be better off.

Suppose you've been dating other men and your children are sulking about it. Women who've gone through this advise that you do not give the kids the idea that they have the right to dictate your social behavior. The best attitude is that you enjoy going out with men your own age, just as you enjoy being with the children. They have their friends, you have yours. If you take this stand it will lessen their initial conviction that you shouldn't be going out with anyone other than their father—and may mitigate the jealousy they feel when you pay attention to someone new.

And remember, if you are going to be you, you have *got* to have a life for yourself. You'll be a better parent if you're not unhappy, frustrated, and bored. Kids turn out better when their mothers have interests other than the children. It's burdensome to a child to feel that his mother lives only through him.

You don't have to overdo it; frequent and prolonged absences from home can really be hurtful to your children. But following the rule of moderation in all things will pan out for you. And it will help if you make some plan for the kids. Let them have a friend to sleep overnight, or—to give you an opportunity to be alone with your new man—let them go to somebody else's house. One last word of caution we hope you don't need: if a romance leads to bed, for heaven's sake—and the kids'—be discreet.

Recommended Reading

The Boys and Girls Book About Divorce by Richard Gardner, M.D. (Bantam Books, paperback, $1.50). Explains aspects of divorce to children age ten and up.

What Every Child Would Like Parents to Know About Divorce by Dr. Lee Salk (Warner Books, paperback, $2.25).

Daddy Doesn't Live Here Anymore by Rita Turow (Greatlakes Living Press, hardbound, $8.95). A teacher/counselor answers the most often asked questions of children.

Children of Divorce by J. Louis Despert (Doubleday, paperback, $2.50).

To help small children understand divorce, ask at your record store for Caedmon Record No. 1362, "Stories About Divorce to Aid Children in Understanding the Situation." Julie Harris and Joseph Wiseman do the dialogue; list price $7.95.

YOUR CHILDREN   DO CHART

ACTION	PRIORITY	DONE	HOW TO
Set up regular meetings to discuss problems			
Assign chores			
Re-evaluate allowances—or their monetary contributions			
Start a record of child expenses			
Arrange for day care			
Arrange car pools			
Note on calendar their father's visiting days			

YOUR CHILDREN   THINK CHART

Has the divorce changed my attitude about them—for better, or for worse?

Am I giving them enough discipline?

Am I spoiling them?

What can they do to help?

Am I giving them enough *quality* time?

Is it necessary for me to talk with teachers, counselors, coaches, club leaders, our minister, priest, or rabbi?

Am I using them as spies?

How are they *really* reacting to the new man in my life?

125

YOUR CHILDREN   THINK CHART

Chapter Nine
YOUR WORK

What is it going to be? It's got to be *some*thing, for both your income and your sanity. In the event you are an heiress (unlikely, or you'd be paying someone else to handle the details in this book for you), you can fill your life with the Assistance League, travel, the hospital guild, and assorted bridge clubs.

This chapter is for the other 99.9 percent of you. Voltaire said, "Work spares us from three great evils: boredom, vice, and need." We're not suggesting you'll begin smuggling dope or diamonds because you have time on your hands, but without a job you *can* be bored, and you can certainly be hungry.

What is your total income now? Is it going to be sufficient in the coming years? Do not count on Harold's continued support, either for you or the children. The ex has a nasty habit of forgetting he used to have a family.

Unless you opt not to work, you fall into one of three categories: (1) you already have a job, (2) you have worked in the past and are now confronted with re-entering the work force, or (3) you have never worked. For all of you, a free booklet, *Careers for Women in the '70s,* may be had by writing for it to the United States Department of Labor, Women's Bureau, 200 Constitution Avenue N.W., Washington, D.C. 20210.

If You Have a Job

Stand back and take a hard look at it. Is there a better job in the firm you can move into? Would additional training or education help you to get the promotion? Think of yourself as a commodity in which you can invest. The more skills you have, the better your opportunity for advancement. If you're stuck in a pin factory tacking heads on pins, it's a hundred to one you'll stay there unless you come up with a better way to stick heads on pins—or any idea that will save money for the firm.

According to business executives, the average woman concentrates on the job at hand and doesn't look to the future. Uncompetitive after long experience as second-class workers, females don't *think* about getting ahead. If you want a promotion, you've got to break the unspoken rule that a woman does not suggest advancement, doesn't ask for a deserved raise. As a group, we tend to just sit there and do as we're told, surrounded by men who are fighting each other tooth and nail for the top positions. The fellows have been taught competition from an early age, whereas we're hidebound in the belief we're only good enough to fix the boss's coffee and soothe his ruffled feathers; i.e., play the wife role.

Many of you could actually do a better job than your boss, but the fact occurs to too few of you. Men don't ordinarily view women as competitors in business (a fact to your advantage), but don't give any man an inkling you aspire to his job . . . particularly your own boss, or you'll find yourself in the unemployment line. The trick is to make him notice your worth and adopt you as his protégé for bigger and better things. Volunteer for special assignments, notice anything that will save the company money, and write a concise memo. Don't go over your boss's head; direct the memo to him. Offer to handle some of his work while he's on vacation. Look at the long view instead of what's under your nose. Change the image you hold of yourself, and begin thinking "career" instead of "job." It is simply a matter of raising your sights.

If you decide your present job is an utter dead end, think about switching. Are you in a field you really like? If so, look for work in a similar business, but with a firm that offers opportunity for advancement. If not, get out of the field. Think about what you'd *like* to do. Take your time on this and wait until you're over the divorce trauma, but consider what kind of work would make you truly happy and involved. Perhaps you've always been interested in medicine—or interior decorating—or hairdressing—or thought you might like to be a librarian. Decide on the field you want and while you're getting your health back, begin putting out feelers. Check the want ads and learn how you can get started, and what is the range of beginning salaries and top salaries. Make deliberate contact with people you know in this area. Cultivate their friendship and subsequent interest in your goal. "It's who you know" is an old and true adage.

It takes courage, sometimes pure guts, to switch jobs for any reason. But if you are sure this is what you want to do and have thoroughly checked out the potential, you'll be grateful you made the move. One note of caution: don't leave one job until you have the second. As the French say, *"On chasse un clou avec un autre"*—we chase one nail with another.

Re-entry

How long has it been? Two years? Twenty years? The longer you've worked at housewifery since your last job, the rougher it seems to face the necessity of finding work.

That supposition, and that alone, is your worst enemy. The fact that you *have* worked outside the home, no matter how long ago, is a distinct advantage over the newly divorced woman who has never worked at all. The next nonsense you must put out of your mind is the thought,

"I'm too old," or "It's too late for me to start again."

In reply to the first thought, a great many people are late bloomers; as youngsters they are bored with their jobs and it's only after the age of thirty that the average woman thinks of herself as a career person. The *thinking* is the trigger that sets her off. George Eliot wrote her first book when in her forties, and we've already prodded you with the reminder of Grandma Moses. With every year you live, you learn, and even closeted as wife and mother, you've certainly picked up a bit of moxie.

Too late to start again? There have been some positive changes since you last worked. In 1972 the Affirmative Action plan went into effect. This means that firms must actively recruit women and minorities, especially for executive positions; they must adhere to this plan before they can be issued a federal contract. Fully one third of American firms has or would like to have federal contracts, so you have a good chance with these companies.

Age is not the drawback it was formerly. Increasingly, employers look for women over forty-five, in the belief that mature women offer more loyalty and certainly are more reliable. There is little possibility that a pregnancy will remove her from the job or that she will take off on a motorcycle with her current lover to live on the shores of Lake Wannahobechoo. Today's young working force is proving, for the most part, to be as steady as a one-legged ladder; and employers are wary of hiring youth (pill or no pill).

On first thought, it would seem sensible to re-enter the same field in which you worked previously. But think further about this. You would be competing with others (perhaps a lot younger) who are thoroughly familiar with newer methods of the business. This sort of thing might dent your self-confidence. It just might be better to apply to all kinds of businesses, emphasizing your talents and skills rather than experience. Besides, your salary of five, ten, or twenty years ago will look paltry today. You might *like* the new field, but if you want to return to the tried and true, you'll have a much better crack at it if you approach it having armed yourself with self-confidence via an interim job.

How to get started? The same way you would had you never worked: the want ads, employment agencies. If you have a field in mind, get a list of the local firms from the Yellow Pages and phone every one of them. If you have a pleasing personality, the phone might be a quicker way to get an interview than a résumé. (Instructions relating to résumés will be given later in this chapter.) We repeat, it's whom you know. So use your friends. Don't beg; merely tell them what you can do in the way of work, the kind of thing you're interested in. Answer want ads with a telegram, which brings immediate attention to your application. Make all sorts of contacts. Do volunteer work . . . at hospitals for children, the senior citizen organization, for underprivileged children. Even if you are not a joiner, JOIN! Join civic groups, political groups, sporting groups. Lots of people have found good (and unrelated) jobs through someone they met on a golf course or at a dog show or a meeting protesting taxes. If you want a job in medicine, tell your doctor and dentist of your interest. If you want to work in law, tell your lawyer. If finance, tell your banker, your tax consultant, your stockbroker.

If You've Never Worked

You will be tempted to take any old job offered you, and will have to if the coffers are empty. But given time, you should land somewhere that's pleasant, even fun . . . and has opportunities for moving up.

First, consider what you *can* do. If your education has encompassed a foreign language, a knowledge of botany, politics, chemistry, literature . . . then apply to firms that need translators, a plant nursery, your assemblyman or congressman, firms dealing in chemicals, libraries. The Yellow Pages are invaluable in this kind of search.

Do you like the idea of outdoor work? This almost automatically puts you in a field traditionally dominated by men. If you love gardening and plants, contact local nurseries. If you like the outdoors *and* exercise, think about delivering mail, a healthy, decently paid job that introduces you to all your neighbors. If you really enjoy driving, how about driving a cab? Small towns often lack cab service, and in many states a license to operate your own cab is not required. (A special license *is* required to drive a bus, but you might think about that, too: a school bus for instance.) In larger cities female cab drivers are on the increase and happily report that they receive higher tips than men drivers.

Consider fields dominated by men. Ninety-six percent of typists are women, but the repair of typewriters is done by ninety-nine men to one woman. And if electricity doesn't turn you gray at the very thought, what's the matter with being an electrician? They average $300 a week. If you like to work with your hands and are athletic as well, think about carpentry, or wallpapering. If mechanical, consider turning into a bona fide mechanic. Welders make an absolute fortune. If you are more interested in humanity than monetary reward, think about training in nursing or with the paramedics.

The federal government has recently funded the Displaced Homemaker Project. These are workshops for women like yourself, assessing your skills and interests and helping you train for the working field. Ask the Information operator if there is a branch in you area.

Perhaps you are creative. If you can make music, turn a fine phrase, take a good picture, or have a flair for making things beautiful, your possibilities are endless.

If you have no specialized education and are not creative in any way except raising kids, mopping floors, and cooking meals—well, there you go—maybe a job in a preschool nursery, domestic work if you can stand it, or the galley in a local restaurant. The one job usually available to unskilled women is that of the waitress. There is a statistic floating around that the average waitress has no husband and something like 3.2 children. Don't kill off the idea, unless you suffer from varicose veins. Most waitresses earn a sizeable income in tips. These jobs may sound menial but even they can lead to better things: e.g., a serious interest in teaching children, the climb from maid to companion-housekeeper (maybe to an old soul who'll leave you half her fortune), or manager of a restaurant.

America is still the land of opportunity, which knocks all the time, but the door is opened only by those who think about getting ahead.

How to Get Ahead

We've told you . . . *think* about it.

You'll have a much better chance if you choose a field in which women are scarce. Sales, finance, construction, manufacturing, science, food . . . all are examples of traditionally masculine careers. If you are in one of these you must learn to handle the sex angle with care. The first rule is never to use your sex, particularly with a man in a higher position. Office sex is so commonplace today that it seldom gets a woman anywhere except, occasionally, out in the cold. On the other hand, do use your femininity. Male coworkers appreciate feminine charm, even an occasional wile, and inasmuch as they don't eye you with suspicion as a competitor, you're more often than not accepted with ease.

The kind of woman they can*not* stand is the tweedy type who wears her clothes like a suit of armor and does a lot of mental shoving. The grace that goes with true femininity, plus good manners, will take you a long way when surrounded by men. You have to hit the mean between bossiness and helplessness. Don't push, but don't be self-effacing either. When you go into a meeting, take the best chair as if it were your right. Above all, don't cry. Never refer to yourself as a woman—you are an architect, a technician, a sales representative. Know your job, do it well, join them for lunch as though you were one of the fellows and keep your conversation on the subject of business. And sports. By all means, read the sports pages; male confreres will appreciate your knowing about Joe Namath and Pete Rose and Tom Watson.

Let's assume you work in an office. Dress correctly and as well as you can afford, but keep it conservative. Do *not* dress the way the secretaries do, even if you are a secretary. No miniskirts, no sandals, no wild hairdos. Look the part of an executive, an executive *woman*. The only male-looking thing you're allowed is a bag resembling an attaché case instead of a feminine purse. The difference in your dress will make you stand out, and when you volunteer for additional responsibility, the thought will click in the male minds that you might well work out in a higher position. You'll certainly be the last woman in the office asked to serve the coffee.

Suppose you are already traveling up the ladder and are in an executive or at least semiexecutive position. Wear a hat to and from the office, and at lunch—you'll be surprised at the effect. A hat makes you look special, giving both an executive and a ladylike aura. When you are traveling on business, the chapeau will effect less hassle about a good room, a good table, and good service.

Your Résumé

A résumé is the very first impression you give to a potential employer. Whether it will open the door to an interview depends on whether it is:

- Neat and well typed. If possible, you should have one hundred printed.
- Concise, to the point. It should not include things employers don't give a damn about—the names of

134

your children, for example, or the fact that your high school yearbook termed you "the prettiest smile."

- Literate. If you make grammatical errors or handle the language badly, you won't be given a first thought.

Here is what a résumé *should* include:

- The type of job you want. Be specific.
- Your skills. List only those applicable to the job.
- Your past accomplishments. List everything you have ever done that gives the impression of authority, whether or not you were paid for it. Use words such as "planned," "designed," "managed," "trained," "edited," "introduced." Skip such terms as "helped," "was involved in." Note dates of your various experience.
- Your education. Degrees received, dates of same, and the school.
- References. Give names of former employers.

Head the résumé with your name, address, phone number. It should be double-spaced, with wide margins to make the résumé more readable, preferably one page.

A helpful hint. Unless you want to be stuck at a typewriter the rest of your working life, do not admit you can type. Good typists are like army sergeants; they are so indispensable that they stay right where they are.

It is advisable also to omit your age. If you do get an interview, you can manage to look younger than you are if the job requires youth. Your work experience and dates will give a clue, but there can be a five-year difference that will give you an advantage. If you worked back in 1935 in a stenographic pool or as a broom pusher in a department store, fail to mention these long-ago and irrelevant chores.

At the end of this chapter is a chart for your notes in working up a résumé.

The Interview

This is your final opportunity to land a job. Appearance is the first impression; unless you're applying for work in the fashion world, do not dress in high style. Conservative is the key word, but keep it feminine. This goes for your hairdo and makeup as well. You are not there to prove how beautiful you are but how skillful, responsible, and sincere.

Unless you are asked, don't volunteer the information that you are divorced. Marital status has nothing to do with ability. If an interviewer inquires, your reply should be brief and to the point; you are now head of a household and responsible for maintaining it. Avoid like the plague any temptation to discuss personal problems.

Appear relaxed and self-assured, giving the impression you can cope with responsibility. If asked about your children's care while you work, have answers ready. Assure the interviewer you have already arranged for their day care, including any emergencies.

Don't let an interview make you nervous. You are not being interrogated by the Almighty; the interviewer is simply a person whose own job it is to fill a position with the best applicant.

Earning at Home

The possibilities are limited, but such a situation is mandatory for those women who feel their children are too young to be left alone . . . or simply cannot bring themselves to farm out the kids on weekdays. You can do telephone solicitation, which can be collection from a firm's debtors or attempting to sell a product or service over the phone. You can type, an occupation that often leads to a job outside the home because you learn about a business or profession as you handle their correspondence and reports. As stated previously, typing is necessary if you want to eat, but it seldom brings advancement. Contact secretarial services for work at home. If you live near a college, leave your name and phone number at the student office in application to type term papers, etc.

If you've always wanted to write, you now have more time—without him around. But be forewarned: the initial income from writing requires much time, perhaps years, and usually involves an ego-smashing number of rejection slips. The same applies to photography and painting . . . any creative field, in fact, in which you are an ingenue.

If you sew, try for contacts at local clothing shops, and do alterations at home. If you have a second language, teach it at home. If you are proficient with any musical instrument, teach that. Ads in the local paper for any of these skills usually bring a heartening batch of inquiries.

If You're Self-Employed

The first rule is to know—thoroughly—not only the field you enter but the *business* of running it. If you open a book store because you love to read, you'll find that at least 70 percent of your time goes into paperwork, and you won't have time to read. Those who have started travel agencies of their own, holding dreams of flying free all around the globe, are so buried by technical chores of planning for customers that they're lucky to get a weekend in Peoria for themselves.

A little tearoom? If it's successful and turns into a restaurant, be prepared to work six and a half days a week. You will never be home on Thanksgiving, Christmas, or Mother's Day. Restaurateurs often joke that when they finally come home their children don't recognize them.

So we begin this subject by warning that going into business for yourself is not all peaches and cream. It is also riddled with pitfalls, one of the most common being that you must be prepared to lose money at least the first year. If the business is to be a success, it will begin to profit only in the second year. Enormous capital is necessary to get started and to hang on until you are in the black. And this may never happen; 80 percent of new businesses collapse within five years.

We are not putting down the idea; small business is the backbone of America. But you must be prepared to raise a great deal of capital, have a liking and a talent for competition, know how to handle finance and credit, and be endowed with incredible stamina and patience.

You should learn the field from A to Z before having your letterhead designed. Many women looking forward to being their own bosses have had the foresight to work in all facets of the specific field, often for a pittance, in order to learn.

If you have even a glimmer of an idea about starting your own business, check with your local library for books on the subject. If you're downright serious, check with your local high school and nearby colleges: many schools offer seminars and night courses on business, marketing, and management. Check your telephone directory to learn if there is a Small Business Administration office in your area. They offer invaluable counsel—and perhaps even a loan for your new venture. SBA was begun by the federal government to give financial and technical assistance to small business.

As we go to press, it has come to our attention that a woman in New York City has begun her own business, called All Systems Go. For a fee she will organize your desk, your files, your closets, your finances. In effect, she will do precisely what we are trying to help you do for yourself —get your life in order. Now that's ingenuity! If you are following our advice and instructions on all cylinders, maybe you can set up your business in your town, and do unto others what you've learned to do for yourself.

Helen Keller wrote, "Security is mostly a superstition. Life is either a daring adventure, or nothing."

So if you want to go it on your own, good luck!

Recommended Reading

Woman's Work Book (Warner Books, paperback, $2.50). How to get your first job, how to re-enter the job market and achieve success. Lists publications, government services, and women's centers.

The Woman's Dress for Success Book by John T. Molloy (Warner Books, paperback, $3.95).

The Managerial Woman by Margaret Hennig and Anne Jardim (Pocket Books, paperback, $2.50).

The Hidden Job Market by Tom Jackson & Davidyne Mayleas (New York Times Books, paperback, $5.95). Information on job hunting; a "system to beat the system."

THINK CHART

YOUR WORK

Thoughts to think

In what fields of work am I skilled?

In what fields of work am I *interested?*

How can I earn money at home?

What can I do in my present job to earn advancement?

How can I earn money part time?

Lists to list

People I know who might help

Employment agencies

Firms in the Yellow Pages

Clothes I need for the job

Groups I should join

YOUR WORK

THINK CHART

NOTES FOR RÉSUMÉ

Chapter Ten
YOUR SOCIAL LIFE

IIIIIⅭ⊃IIIIIIIIIIIⅭ⊃IIIIIIIIIIⅭ⊃IIIIIIIIIⅭ⊃IIIIIIⅭ⊃IIIIIIIIIⅭ⊃IIIIIIIIIⅭ⊃IIIIIIIIⅭ⊃IIIIIIIⅭ⊃IIIIIIIIIⅭ⊃III

We've already suggested that you rid yourself of the idea you are a weirdo because you're divorced. The world doesn't think so; why should you? Divorced people are no longer considered misfits except by the most hidebound souls. Politicians in high places have been divorced; so, even, have those in the ministry. You have plenty of company as a single parent . . . one out of every six children in the United States lives with a single parent.

And lest you feel guilty about being at work when the kids come home from school, know that more than one half of American children have mothers who work. According to the Women's Bureau of the United States Department of Labor, only one out of six American households has a father who goes to work and a mother who stays home all day.

You are now your own person, with enormous opportunity to build a new social life as well as a career. You will find a new source of warmth and support from other women, especially other divorcees. And part of this camaraderie will stem from your married friends, who now suddenly come to you with confidences about the unhappiness of their own marriages. They come for comfort and advice . . . and the basic reason they now reveal their misery to you is because *you* have taken the step and they admire your courage and have need of your understanding.

You'll also find out who are your friends. A few will side with your former husband; most of these will have been his business friends and those people he's known all his life. But the ones who stand behind you will be the jewels in your crown. You should take time and trouble for their care and feeding; they are going to make your future life infinitely more enjoyable.

Your own relatives will of course side with you. But what about your former in-laws? If you are genuinely fond of Harold's mother and father, by all means keep them in your life. If you don't like them, cast them out—*unless* you have children. These people have a moral right to watch their grandchildren grow up, and you would be a bit of a heel to deny them this. You don't have to have the old folks over for dinner, but you *can* deliver and pick up the kids at their home.

Your neighbors? Same thing. The solution of your former marital woes is none of their business so, unless they are true friends, keep your own counsel with neighbors.

It's possible that when you attend church or go to a PTA meeting you'll notice other women looking at you a bit longer than is polite. Your first thought: "They disapprove." Well, forget that, because most of them are looking at you with envy. Would to God *they* could change their lives the way you have.

In business, of course, you will find much social intercourse and, as always, the choice is up to you. The one burr under the saddle may be the attitude of women married to your colleagues. As married women take a dim view of the single females working with or for their husbands, they may regard you as a threat. So when you are in the company of these women be your charming self, but appear asexual. Keep your attitude matter-of-fact, even if their husbands have been pinching you behind the file cabinet. Talk to them as friends and they will be your friends.

You will make a lot of new ones if you indulge yourself in new interests. You should definitely become a joiner. There are groups all over the place offering support to

144

divorced women, in colleges, churches, synagogues. Newspapers feature many clubs and workshops devoted to helping the divorcee. Parents Without Partners is a fine organization, and you are eligible regardless of the age of your children. There are one thousand chapters of PWP throughout the United States and if none is listed in your phone directory, write Parents Without Partners at 7910 Woodmont Avenue, Washington D.C. 20014, for the address of the chapter nearest you. For $18, you can join the National Association of Divorced Women, 200 Park Avenue, New York, New York 10017, (212) 344-8407. This association offers answers to legal, financial, employment and psychological problems. There is Divorce-Aide, a New York-based organization with six-week workshop sessions for a minimal fee, 521 Fifth Avenue, New York, New York 10017 (212) 369-3966. You can join or found a NEXUS group and participate in rap sessions, lectures, parties, etc. Address is P. O. Box 176, Garden City, New York 11530. The grandmother of them all is NOW (National Organization for Women), and a chapter is near you wherever you live. NOW offers all sorts of help, as well as opportunity for new interests.

Here is a list of activities for you to consider. Many are social, but some may well lead to a job.

> Museum membership
> A second language (or third)
> Politics. A wide field embracing work for your candidate and involvement in tax reform, water quality, etc.
> Gourmet cooking
> Auto repair
> Seminars on writing
> Home decoration
> Stamp or coin collecting
> Tennis
> A course in travel agency work

Flying
Seminars on investment
Bowling
A course in nursing
A musical instrument. Is there a small orchestra in your
    town?
Sailing
Folk dancing
Golf
Invite foreign students to your home for dinner
Skiing
Crewel
Mosaics
Join in a hospital guild
Join an art association
    Work for children (the deaf, blind, mentally re-
    tarded, day care centers)

The above list is varied, with something for everybody.
If you like to work with your hands and are creative, here's
another list of interests that will enrich your life and make
new friends.

Decoupage	Rug making
Ceramics	Knitting
Jewelry	Basketry
Soft sculpture	Chinese brush work
Batik	on paper and clay
Crocheting	Weaving
Quilting	Spinning and dyeing
Wood carving	Tapestry
Woodworking	Glass
Stoneware	Leather crafts
Porcelain	Stained glass
Raku	Metalworking
Caning	Bookbinding
Picture framing	Patchwork
Upholstery	Appliqué

Papier-mâché
Collage
Rope sculpture
Stone carving
Dressmaking

Enameling
Bronze casting
Handcrafted miniatures
Puppet making and
   puppetry

Holidays

Christmas and Thanksgiving are the roughest. The rest hold fewer memories and are not usually associated with family. Surely you can get through the Fourth of July by yourself, and as for New Year's Eve, who needs it?

You should not be by yourself on Christmas and Thanksgiving. Going "home," we have learned, is the best idea by far. To be a daughter and sister again, to experience the nostalgia of girlhood ties, will strengthen your conviction about who you are.

If you have no old family homestead, not even a family, do plan to leave town. There's nothing more depressing, whatever one's situation, than to decorate a Christmas tree and then sit there looking at it, alone. Tie up with another single friend and go away for the holidays . . . to a skiing resort or, if in a suitable climate, a golf or tennis resort. Or take your children to such places; there they'll have other children to play with and won't miss old Dad. If you have no children and can't dig up an enthusiastic friend, perhaps you belong to a club that has plans for a holiday trip. Another choice, and not a bad one at all, is scanning the paper for trips planned exclusively for singles by travel agencies. You are bound to make new friends on such a jaunt.

Dining Alone

In public, this can be excruciating for a woman. We know one who says she's sure other diners think she's a hooker. Another, vice president of an oil company, is a staunch advocate of the hat ploy. She says a hat makes you look above it all and *feel* above it all. Further, a hat somehow commands immediate respect from the maitre d', who will think twice before he seats you by the kitchen door. And it helps dispel the idea that women are rotten tippers. We don't want to run the idea of a hat into the ground, but it *is* symbolic of the attitude you should present, i.e. "I'm *some*body, and don't you dare try to put me down."

Tell him, "One, please." Don't be apologetic because you are alone.

If you project an aura of meekness and humility, you can bet you'll wait fifteen minutes for a menu, twenty minutes for your martini, thirty minutes for your first course, and an hour for your bill. If you suspect this is the way it's going to be, there's a perfectly lovely way to draw the attention of the staff. You rise from your chair, gather your belongings, and sweep toward the exit. In nothing flat, you'll be surrounded by fawning waiters.

Even if the service is good, the period between ordering and being served your first course is interminable when dining alone. Almost everyone else is gazing into eyes across a table for two, or in rollicking groups of four or six. The answer to this is to rivet your attention on the "old marrieds." They are easily spotted—they're the ones who stare into space as they stuff their faces, and their only conversation consists of, "Pass the salt." Now *you*, you can busy yourself with a book or newspaper, or work from the office.

Finally, do not overtip. The waiter will take this as a sign of apology and you have nothing to apologize for. You've very probably enjoyed your meal more than the old marrieds, who ran out of conversation ten years ago.

Men

Ah, men! To some of us, they are necessary to have around or we feel like half a human being. If you are the

148

type who simply can't go it alone, watch out for the disease known as reboundities. The danger of rebound is now imminent, but you well know that anything done too quickly is usually done badly.

You mustn't expect the immediate miracle of a brand new man in your life. In nineteen out of twenty cases, Mr. Right is not standing in the wings. In one out of twenty, he's already been there for some time. But chances are you'll find those bachelors you've known for years are not going to inundate you suddenly with flowers, gifts, and dinner dates.

You've got to plan how to meet new men. And the very best way is those new interests we've been advocating. Unless you are enamored of the milkman, mailman, or your plumber, staying home is going to keep you as chaste as you are.

We shall now get into sex. And right out of it, because we face the fact that no one can advise another about her sex life. It's your own affair (pun intended) and we're not about to meddle in it. You simply have to consider your physical needs, your conscience, and your discretion . . . and go your own way. By now you're a big girl, you know what makes babies, you know what your mother told you, you're no longer a virgin (we hope). You may be sex-starved, but you ought to know by now that sex can be a glorious and fulfilling experience but, emotionally, it can also open a can of worms.

(Here we must issue a warning about climbing into the hay with your estranged husband—a fairly common practice. In bygone years, many state laws included something called condonation. The upshot of condonation is that once a marriage partner has sued for divorce, the initial waiting period begins with the most recent date sexual intercourse took place between the couple. From then on, sex is taboo; should it happen again, the starting date is moved forward to *that* date. So if your newly departed husband wants to return to the bedroom *and* objects to the divorce, beware.

149

He can legally postpone the final decree with each romp. By now, condonation has been wiped off the books of many states, particularly those with no-fault divorce. But the law still lurks in some states, so check it out, madame.)

Suppose you've met another man, perhaps on a business trip, in a college course, in community work, or in the job change you've made to a male-staffed office. If you have given honest thought to your own failings in your recent marriage, you'll know that honesty is the best policy. This time, you don't have to play games, you don't have to gain his approval by striving to please. You can simply be yourself. And if you are, you'll be in the current swing of things.

If your marriage was one of considerable length (as example, if your wedding gift *The Joy of Cooking* has lost its spine), you will experience a certain shock at the new attitudes of men today. The average man no longer goes for shrinking violets. Rather, he is attracted to a woman in control of her life and of herself. He no longer likes the helpless type, which he translates as "Poor me, I need someone strong to take care of me." (Unless, of course, he too is weak-willed; like attracts like.) Above all, he can't abide tears. Do not babble to him about the trials of your marriage and divorce.

The only male attitude still unchanged is the assumption that you have stored up so much sexual energy that you will hurl him onto your bed at first opportunity. As we've said, your choice. But today's man looks on an affair as something in which he has no responsibility whatever . . . there are no strings . . . possessiveness is o-u-t . . . jealousy is unthinkable. He can have an affair with you, and with as many others as he pleases. You, on the other hand, may retain the old-fashioned notion that sex requires true love. Well, welcome to today's new man.

You don't have to marry him and probably won't—at least for a while. Statistics show that divorced women stay single longer than divorced men, who, as we've written, can't bear life without a housekeeper. The divorced woman of today thinks harder as well as longer about remarriage, knowing full well that marriage is the easiest thing in the world to get into . . . and the hardest thing to get out of.

Given time, you probably will remarry—four out of five divorcees do. You may not, from choice, because you have found that your single life offers you an aliveness that you much prefer to an existence in tandem.

If you stay single *against* your will, we have a statistic that might cheer you. According to a recent time study, the average husband offers fourteen minutes of conversation each day. For the reward of that much communication, is it worth the hassle?

YOUR SOCIAL LIFE

THINK CHART

Thoughts to think	*Lists to list*
Where and when shall I make my first step and go somewhere alone?	My friends
How about that list of hobbies in the text? Which of them appeal to me?	Groups to join
What shall I do this Christmas?	Places I want to go
Do I really *want* to start something with this new man?	

YOUR SOCIAL LIFE   THINK CHART

Chapter Eleven

YOUR MOVING

IIIIIC3IIIIIIIIIIC3IIIIIIIIIIC3IIIIIIIIIIC3IIIIIIIIIIC3IIIIIIIIIIC3IIIIIIIIIIC3IIIIIIIIIIC3IIIIIIIIIIC3III

It's a backbreaker.

It's an emotional wrench, especially if you are leaving a home you have loved but must forfeit because of finances or because he demands half the proceeds.

It's a pit for the budget if you don't choose the right moving firm.

It's nervous breakdown time. You could have inherited a million dollars and been voted Miss America, but you are still heading into a maelstrom that can make your teeth jump.

With all those dire warnings out of the way, let us now assure you that with careful attention to this chapter, you will sail through the storm as easily as possible. We shall give it all to you, chronologically, beginning with a reminder to gradually consume the food stored in your freezer.

We'll assume you've found the new place. *Before* you pay rent or arrange an escrow, check out your current lease if you have one. People tend to take for granted a thirty-day notice, but there is the hidden horror of leases requiring a sixty-day notice. Don't get stuck with a continuing lease via this oversight; if you have a landlord/lady, be sure to give him/her the required notice. Have your security and cleaning deposits returned to you. In some states, owners must pay interest on these deposits. Get back any deposits with utility companies. Then make plans for your moving date, and enroll the kids in school if necessary.

What to Move

Decide now what things you will move, and what you will give away or sell. This can save you considerably. There's no sense in paying good money to move a chair with broken springs, the heavy popover pan you never use, the books you didn't enjoy and will certainly never read again. The former can go to your local thrift shop. Get a receipt; such donations are tax deductible. The books will be welcome at nursing homes or your local library. So make your give-away list, which should include everything you think won't sell at a garage sale, or things you'd like to give for free out of the goodness of your heart.

STORAGE?

If you plan to put anything in storage, check your insurance policy to learn if such items will be covered while in storage. Also, for anything taken to storage on moving day, make an itemized list of such things and have it signed by the moving men.

THE GARAGE SALE

You will probably have two. One before you move and one after, because no matter how hard you work at the pile for the premove sale, you'll find when unpacking that there's even more stuff you don't need. Have your first garage sale well in advance of moving day; get rid of everything before you begin packing. Weekends are best, of course, and start it on a Friday if you can—that extra day will bring the dealers and bargain buffs who show up early. Wait until Sunday afternoon before desperation time, when you reduce prices on what's left. In addition to the early birds, there are vultures who purposely wait for the time you lower prices.

How to price things? Float through a few garage sales in the neighborhood to get an idea of what other people charge. Don't price things too low, because the average drive-in customer will give you an argument anyway.

What to include? Everything you don't want. Do not think, "Nobody in their right mind would want *that*." It's amazing but true that the junk sells better than the good stuff. You can offer a Royal Doulton cup and saucer that will just sit there, while Johnny's broken kite and Samantha's beat-up ski jacket will sell in the first hour. The only things you do *not* include are those you have a sneaking suspicion might be valuable. Have these appraised, either by a good antique dealer or one of those serendipity shops specializing in nostalgia.

Don't allow strangers to enter your home. It's a good idea to have a man around so that you don't broadcast "single" signals.

Advertise the sale in your local paper—and have the kids post signs at vantage points and supermarkets in the neighborhood.

Make Your Floor Plan

Know not only what you want moved, but where you want it placed in your new home. There's nothing more time-wasting (expensive) and ultimately more frustrating than standing within the bare walls of your new home trying to decide where to put the desk—while the moving men stand there holding the desk. There is a lovely way to avoid this.

Take measurements of every room in the new place and include the location of windows, doors, and closets. Now, on a large sheet of white paper, make an outline of each room in the house or apartment. Draw it to a scale of one-quarter inch to one foot, noting the doors, windows, and closets. There is your floor plan. Now, measure the furniture that will be moved and make a list of each piece and its size. Next, using colored paper, make a pencil outline of each item. (A king-size bed is six by seven feet; therefore, its scale model will be one and one half inches by one and three quarters inches.) Cut these out and label them—club chair, kitchen table, etc—then play with them on your floor plan. Couch here, coffee table in front; is there room enough between the coffee table and the chair across the room?

We admit the preparation of this game can be a slight bore, but do it well ahead of time, perhaps on a rainy Sunday. Once you have all the pieces, arranging the furniture ahead of time can be fun and will most certainly save time on moving day. Time is what they charge you for in a local move. Do not file the plan away. Make a Xerox copy for the driver, and keep both original and copy with your jewelry and other valuables you'll be transporting yourself.

Prepare the New Home

As soon as it is emptied of former residents, get yourself over there with the following: broom, brush, rags, wet mop, dry mop, bucket, all purpose cleaner, disposable cleaning gloves, paper towels, window cleaner, floor wax, and mop for same. Shelf paper, thumb tacks, scissors. And your kids to help. A thermos of iced tea, lemonade, or hot coffee, depending on weather, and fruit and a couple of sandwiches for fuel. If you have no little helpers, maybe a radio to keep you company.

Knowing the place is ready for the movers puts a good part of the battle behind you.

The Time to Move

Few of us have the choice but if you do, try not to move in summer months. This is the time most people move and as a result, you don't always have your choice of moving day. More important, you have less assurance the movers will arrive at your new home when promised. Avoid weekends, which often involve overtime, thus extra cost.

Choosing the Mover

It could be *you*. But only if you have strong sons and/or muscular friends. U-Haul or Ryder will be your sole bill, which will include the gas used (these vehicles get only five to ten miles per gallon). You won't lose anything or have to worry about theft, you will drive carefully over bumps to save that antique mirror, you will be in charge of arrival time, and you will save a great deal of money. A cautionary note: be sure sons and friends know how to pack the vehicle —everything firmly secure to prevent shifting. A few basic hints: big appliances go in first; tables go in upside down with a blanket or rug underneath. Pack small things in all empty spaces, put cartons of breakables on top, slide rolled rugs along the sides, and stand anything glass *on end*, not flat.

There's a small chance your employer is paying for the move, relative to a job shift. In this case you are responsible, so check it out with the personnel department of your firm and learn what the procedure should be. Keep all receipts: a large portion of cost to you is tax-deductible when a move is job-related.

There's a bigger chance it's all in your own lap. Keep in mind, therefore, that a great many people have decided to make money in the moving business. The big ones are Allied Van Lines, Aero Mayflower Transit, North American Van Lines, Bekins Van Lines, United Van Lines, Atlas Van Lines, Global Van Lines, and Lyon Moving and Storage. All these large firms register their rates—which are very similar —with the Interstate Commerce Commission. The ICC regulates prices for some intrastate carriers as well as all interstate movers. You'll pay about the same price for licensed carriers, but beware the "scabs" who resurrect a truck from somewhere and have no insurance against loss or breakage. Some women have succumbed to the low estimate of a scab, watched the van move out of the driveway with every material thing they own—and have never seen any of it again. Often scabs will give an estimate, maybe five hundred dollars, and then when you hoist pen to write out a check at your new door, tell you the bill is sixteen hundred dollars because your stuff wasn't packed right, the distance was more than they figured, there were too many steps, or your house was eighty yards back from the street. Any excuse, but there you are, having agreed to pay C.O.D.—and stuck.

This can happen with professional movers, who are not bound by law to their estimates, but it can be avoided if you are careful to list everything to be moved and tell them of any possible difficulties at the new place—including elevators. Professional carriers attempt honest estimates; they have to because the ICC is, to be explicit, watching their every move.

Get at least three estimates. Consult friends who may have recommendations. Phone the Better Business Bureau to learn if any complaints have been lodged against the carriers you are considering. Be careful in your choice, knowing that movers much prefer jobs paid for by firms moving employees. This means repeat business for them, so their hearts are in these jobs. C.O.D. customers don't receive nearly the same tender care. And single people such as yourself have much less to move than offices or large families . . . a dearth which often means space waste or labor problems for moving firms and therefore higher cost to you. Be wary and business-like with your estimator, and be honest. Tell him how many steps the men will have to ascend and descend, if there are narrow passageways and what access there might be (or not be) for your grand piano. Know that long-distance moving is usually paid for by the pound per mile, and local moving is based on time.

Once you've made your choice of carrier, consider insurance. Big firms carry insurance but it is based on weight, at approximately sixty cents per pound. Therefore, if you own a tiny Titian, you need to take out additional insurance (at five dollars per thousand-dollar value), and the company representative will arrange this for you. On second thought, if you have a tiny Titian, you'd better put it in your tote bag on moving day along with your dollars and diamonds.

Get from the mover a copy of the ICC's *Red Book*, a summary of information for shippers of household goods. The mover is obligated to give you this, plus three other booklets devoted to advice on moving.

Set your pickup and delivery dates with him, including time of day as accurately as is possible. Have him put these in writing on the Order of Service and bill of lading.

Packing

Professional movers will pack for you and do it with expertise, but it costs. Also expensive are the packing boxes they can provide, but these are worth it . . . much less trouble than running through supermarkets to lug home empty cartons. Furthermore, every box you use for packing must have a lid that can be secured. Carriers' cartons are made to order and can be kept for future moves. They also have wardrobe crates, replete with sturdy rod across the top, a worthy investment for your clothes.

Don't pack any one carton to a weight heavier than fifty pounds if you can avoid it. Nor should you confront Herculean moving men with scores of dinky little boxes.

Begin by packing the things you use least. A suggested order: books, files, scrapbooks, records, tapes. (Books might be mailed at special fourth-class book rate—as of this writing, cheaper if your move costs by weight.) Then the stuff on the top shelves in your kitchen: vases, tureens, etc. Bed, bath, and kitchen linens and towels. Everything off the walls (some carriers sell skinny boxes for pictures and mirrors). Wrap table legs in newspaper. Take down the curtains, wash and dry them, stuff them in available drawer space. Such space can also be filled with soft things—purses, sweaters, shoes, but nothing too heavy to tax the strength of the drawers. Then glassware and china, pots and pans. Save some of these and put in a special box to go with you to the new abode. You'll be living out of this box for a couple of days. Pack up the bathroom, saving accessories for the "special" box.

Each dish, cup, etc. should be wrapped in scrunched newspaper. Flat dishes should be placed in a vertical position. Pack lampshades one inside the other, in large cartons. Roll up smaller rugs and tie at middle and ends. Leave mattress covers on mattresses and slipcovers on furniture as protection during the moving.

Countdown (in the calm before the storm)

MOVING DAY MINUS THREE

- Send change-of-address cards, available at the post office, to all people listed on the name-change chart.
- Notify the proper sources to discontinue on moving day your newspaper, milk delivery, fuel, water, electricity, laundry. Order phone disconnected the day *after* moving day.
- If you have rugs, drapes, or furniture to be cleaned, or furniture to be reupholstered, this is the day to have them picked up if you're moving locally. Delivery at your new place will save the cost of moving them.
- Pick up all laundry and dry cleaning.
- Eat from pantry shelves. Who needs the cost of moving cans of tuna fish and soup?

MOVING DAY MINUS TWO

- Tape all movable parts of appliances. As example, the pickup arm of your record turntable.
- Eat leftovers in the fridge.
- Defrost the fridge and freezer.
- If your new place is within reasonable driving distance, take your plants there. Carriers will not move plants.

161

- Clean your fridge and freezer thoroughly.
- Stuff the fridge and freezer, when dry, with soft goods. The washer and dryer can also be filled with towels, blankets, sheets, etc.
- Tie or tape every carton you have packed so that they are securely closed.
- Label each carton with (1) the room where the movers are to place it and (2) what is in it. You'll be grateful for the latter when you start unpacking.

(Do *not* pack things you will need to clean your old place after the moving men have denuded it down to the walls. Leave mops, scrubbing equipment, etc. in your kitchen for last-minute cleanup.)

- If you are moving a considerable distance, pack a suitcase with the clothes you will need for several days. Pretend it's a suitcase for a trip to the moon. You'll need hairbrush, comb, toothbrush, toothpaste, bath towel, soap, pills, tampons, toilet tissue, paper towels. Some of this can go into the "special" box, along with candles and matches in case the electricity hasn't been turned on, and a couple of light bulbs in case it has. Put in a saucepan or two, frying pan, kettle, hammer and pliers, scissors, dishes, and utensils you'll need until you're unpacked. Tea bags or instant coffee to sustain you, fruit, crackers and cheese. A can of martini mix may save your life tomorrow.
- Get cash, a cashier's check, money order, or certified check for the amount of the estimate, and put it in your purse.
- Put the floor plans in your purse.

Moving Out Day

Make coffee out of your "special" box, then sit around and go crazy while you wait for the movers to arrive. You can disconnect appliances while you wait; some movers charge for this, believe it or not. You might also give your dog or cat a tranquilizer to forestall additional nervous breakdowns.

When the van gets there, stick close to the head man as he checks off the things loaded. Be particularly interested if he marks something as already damaged, to make sure you agree with him.

If this is a move of fifty miles or more (when cost is figured by weight), try to be charming when you suggest you will follow the van to the weighing scale. It is standard procedure for a moving van to be weighed before and after loading in a long distance move. Ergo, it's a wise precaution to check out the *final* figure, and one recommended by the ICC.

As a parting gesture, give the driver his copy of your floor plan, plus a phone number where you may be reached if he's toting your worldly goods to another city. And assure him you'll be at your new place when he arrives.

Moving In Day

Be sure you *are* there. They'll sometimes wait for a couple of hours, after which they haul everything to a storage warehouse. For which you have to pay. One woman we know was tied up in a freeway accident on moving day, and when she finally arrived at her new home, the movers (a small-potato outfit) had stowed everything in the garage . . . and left. She slept that night on the side of a couch with her face in the open window of her clothes dryer, which was stuffed with her son's shoes.

Pray they get there when they've promised. In long-distance moves the van is frequently late, sometimes as much as a week. Movers must notify you if they'll be delayed but, nonetheless, in the interim you have to sleep somewhere and live out of your suitcase and that all-important box.

Now that they're there, inspect everything carefully. If anything is damaged or missing, note same on the driver's shipping order before you sign his receipt. This will serve as support for your formal claim to be made later. If you haven't opportunity to check everything, note on his bill of lading, "Final settlement pending further inspection."

Even if you've hired a major moving firm, the final bill *may* be more than the estimate. A 1970 rule of the ICC states that the driver can extract from you only 10 percent of any additional cost. (You have fifteen days to pay the remainder.) Another ICC ruling: it is illegal for movers to solicit a tip. This doesn't say they won't take one, but it's interesting that, according to the head of a major carrier, "Rich people seldom tip."

If you have a gripe of any sort, you can report it to the ICC at Household Goods Branch, Interstate Commerce Commission, 12th and Constitution Avenue, Washington, D.C. 20423. The toll-free number is (800) 424-9312.

We leave you, by candlelight or a single bulb, with your canned martini and 8,304,959 cartons. Guess who gets to *un*pack? But cheer up . . . a new home is *really* a new life for you.

Recommended Reading

Did Somebody Pack the Baby? By Barbara Friedrich and Sally Hultstrand (Prentice-Hall, hardbound, $8.95). Even if you have your move well in hand, this one's fun to read.

Do It Yourself Moving by George Sullivan (Collier/Macmillan, paperback, $3.95). For those of you who choose to do it "on the cheap."

DO CHART

YOUR MOVING

ACTION	PRIORITY	DONE	HOW TO
Check current lease for required notice	1		
Get back security/cleaning deposits	1		
Get back deposits on utilities	1		
Start eating food stored in freezer			
Decide what to move, sell, store, give away			Use the Think Chart
Check if items to be stored will be covered by insurance			
Garage sale			See text
Make scale floor plan of new place			See text
Clean, prepare the new place			
Choose the mover			See text. Get three estimates
Set the date, and time of day			
Enroll children in new school			
Is additional insurance necessary?			
Start eating pantry foods			

YOUR MOVING   DO CHART

ACTION	PRIORITY	DONE	HOW TO
Wash curtains, stow in drawers			
Send rugs to cleaners			
Send furniture to be reupholstered			
Pick up laundry and dry cleaning			
Start "box of necessaries"			See text
Pack suitcase			See text
Packing			See text
Give notice to discontinue			
Newspaper			
Milk			
Fuel service			
Electricity			
Water			
Gas			
Telephone			
Cable TV			

YOUR MOVING   DO CHART

ACTION	PRIORITY	DONE	HOW TO
Fill out change-of-address card for post office			
Take plants to new place			
Eat leftovers in fridge			
Defrost fridge and freezer			See text
Label all cartons			
Get check or cash for mover			
Put valuables in purse			
Moving Day			
Tranquilize your dog, cat			
Oversee driver's damage reports			
Give driver copy of your floor plan			See text
Oversee report of weighing			See text
Give driver phone number where you can be reached			
On arrival, check for loss or damage			See text

167

YOUR MOVING THINK CHART

To be stored

To be given away

For garage sale

INDEX